Authors in Their Age

WORDSWORTH

Authors in Their Age

WORDSWORTH

Anthony Adams

BLACKIE

BLACKIE & SON LTD
Bishopbriggs Glasgow G64 2NZ
Furnival House 14-18 High Holborn London WC1V 6BX

Cover portrait of Wordsworth by B. R. Haydon
reproduced by courtesy of the National Portrait Gallery, London

Printed in Great Britain by
Thomson Litho Ltd., East Kilbride, Scotland

Authors in Their Age

Authors in Their Age is a series of introductions to the work of major authors in English literature. Each book provides the background information that can help a reader see such an author in context, involved in and reacting to the society of which he was a part.

Some volumes are devoted to individual authors such as Chaucer and Wordsworth. Others look at a particular period in our literary history in which an author can be seen as representative of his time—for example, *The Age of Keats and Shelley* and *The Age of Lawrence.*

There is no attempt to impose a standard format on each of the books. However, all the books provide biographical material and deal with the important political, social and cultural movements of the time. Each book considers the author's readership, the problems of editing his or her work and the major influences on his or her writing. All are well illustrated with drawings, documents or photographs of the time.

There is also a guide to further reading and other source material which will enable the student to progress to a more detailed study of the writer's work and its treatment by literary critics.

Anthony Adams
Esmor Jones
General Editors

Contents

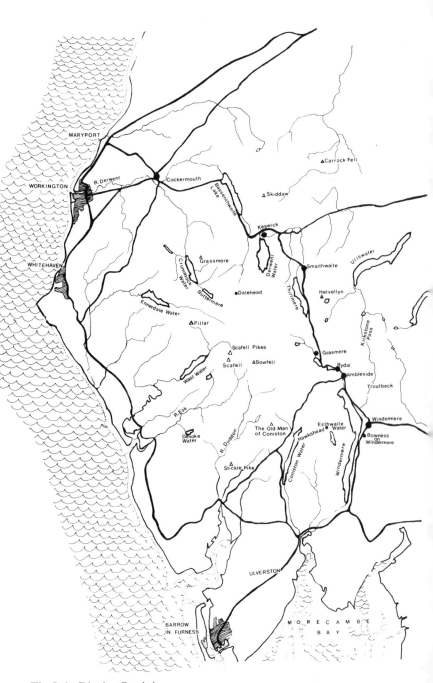

The Lake District, Cumbria

I

Towards a Biography

This introductory chapter does not pretend to be an adequate biography of an exceedingly complex person. There are already plenty of sources for those who want to know the full story of Wordsworth's life. But some consideration of it is essential if we are to begin to understand his work. More than most poets, his work reflects the life of its creator—'*My life is in my writings*', as he himself put it. Certainly his most ambitious and successful poem, *The Prelude*, was generally spoken of by him as '*the Poem of my own Life*' and he also left his *Autobiographical Memoranda* that he dictated to his brother, Christopher Wordsworth, in 1847. But, inevitably, his writings have doubts attached to them as true sources of a knowledge of his life and thought. It is almost impossible for the most modest of us to write our autobiography without wanting to present ourselves in the best possible light, and modesty was not a virtue that one would normally attribute to Wordsworth. *The Prelude* remains a fascinating study of how Wordsworth saw himself, his record of himself for future generations, but it is far from being the plain and unvarnished truth. To understand this poem, therefore, as well as many of his other works, some acquaintance with the main events in Wordsworth's life is essential and this chapter is intended as a starting point. It will concentrate upon those events and aspects of his personality that seem to be of particular importance for understanding his writings.

I

Let us start where his contemporaries did, with the appearance of the man himself. The best of many sources of information on this point is the account written by Thomas de Quincey in 1834, recalling his first visit to Wordsworth in 1807:

> [He] *was, upon the whole, not a well made man. His legs were pointedly condemned by all female-connoisseurs in*

legs; not that they were bad in any way which would force itself upon your notice—there was no absolute deformity about them ... But the worst part of Wordsworth's person was the bust; there was a narrowness and a droop about the shoulders which became striking, and had an effect of meanness, when brought into close juxtaposition with a figure of more statuesque build ... the total effect of (his) person was always worst in a state of motion. Meantime, his face—that was one which would have made amends for greater defects of figure ... It was a face of the long order ... The head was well filled out ... The forehead was not remarkably lofty ... but it is, perhaps, remarkable for its breadth and expansive development. Neither are the eyes of Wordsworth 'large' ... on the contrary they are (I think) rather small; but that does not interfere with their effect, which at all times is fine, and suitable to his intellectual character ... his eyes are not, under any circumstances, bright, lustrous, or piercing; but after a long day's toil in walking, I have seen them assume an appearance the most solemn and spiritual that it is possible for the human eye to wear. The light which resides in them is at no time a superficial light; but, under favourable accidents, it is a light which seems to come from unfathomed depths: in fact, it is more truly entitled to be held 'the light that never was on land or sea', a light radiating from some far spiritual world, than any of the most idealising that ever yet a painter's hand created.[1]

At the same time de Quincey noted an astonishing resemblance between the face of Wordsworth and that of Milton according to some portraits that he had seen, a comparison that Wordsworth himself was also apt to make in other connections. Certainly he was a striking man, as much to his neighbours at Grasmere as to his fellow writers. With his lifelong liking for long walks, during which he would compose, talking quietly to himself all the time, he speedily earned a reputation for eccentricity. One of his neighbours is reported as saying of him: '*He goes bumbling and muffling, and talking to hissen, but whiles he's as sensible as you or me.*' He was also exceedingly tall for the time, a fact that is frequently observed in contemporary accounts.

With this striking appearance went an equally striking personality. As we shall have occasion to note many times, he

Detail from a portrait of Wordsworth by Benjamin Robert Haydon, 1818 (National Portrait Gallery, London)

Detail from a portrait of Milton aged 21 by an unknown artist (National Portrait Gallery, London)

was nothing if not egotistical and he found it difficult to forgive a real or imagined injury or a bad review. So much so, in fact, that his sister and wife, both of whom adored and spoiled him, had to smuggle the journals containing reviews into his cottage before he caught sight of them. He saw himself in a poetic, as well as a physical sense, as someone who had a strong resemblance to Milton and in this he was much encouraged by his friend Coleridge. Although he was originally expected to go into the Church as a profession, it seems as if it was at the early age of 14 that he made a conscious decision that he was to be a Poet, a decision that was strongly reinforced while he was an undergraduate at Cambridge. He describes how he underwent a moment of dedication when, walking in the early morning, he was struck by the beauty of the sunrise:

> *My heart was full; I made no vows, but vows*
> *Were then made for me; bond unknown to me*
> *Was given, that I should be, else sinning greatly,*
> *A dedicated Spirit.*[2]

His sister, Dorothy, had some misgivings about this at the time. In a letter written just after William had taken his somewhat undistinguished degree at Cambridge she says:

> *William, you may have heard, lost the chance (indeed the*
> *certainty) of a fellowship, by not combating his inclinations.*
> *He gave way to his natural dislike to studies so dry as many*
> *parts of mathematics, consequently could not succeed at*
> *Cambridge ... William has a great attachment for poetry*
> *... which is not the most likely thing to produce his*
> *advancement in the world.*

He regularly refers to himself in his work, in even the most trivial contexts, as a Poet, and always with a capital initial letter. Even of his loved (and lovely) garden at Grasmere he writes somewhat self-consciously and without any shade of irony: '*A Poet made it*'. An inability to take himself other than seriously was a limitation of his character that was often commented upon by those who knew him. The comments by his neighbours at Rydal in his later years are typical: '*You could tell fra the man's face his potry would niver have no laugh in it ... I don't remember he ever laughed in his life, he'd smile times or two.*'

These remarks are quoted from a conversation recorded in 1870 by Canon H. D. Rawnsley and were included in a paper to

the Wordsworth Society in 1882 and the whole passage is worth
quoting for its vivid picture of the poet in his last years:

> '*Now tell me,' said I, 'what was the poet like in face and
> make?' '. . . He was much to look at like his son William; he
> was a listy [lusty] man was his son, mind ye. But for a' he
> was a sizeable man, was the father, he was plainish
> featured, and was a man as had no pleasure in his faace.
> Quite different Wudsworth was from li'le Hartley.*[3] *Hartley
> always had a bit of smile or twinkle in his faace, but
> Wudsworth was not lovable in the faace by noa means, for
> o' he was a sizeable man, mind ye' . . .*
>   '*Was he', I said, 'a sociable man, Mr. Wordsworth, in
> the earliest times you can remember?'*
>   '*Wudsworth, . . . for a' he had noa pride nor nowt, was a
> man who was quite one to hissel, ye kna. He was not a man
> as folks could crack* [chat] *wi', nor not a man as could crack
> wi' folks. But there was another thing as kep' folks off, he
> had a ter'ble girt deep voice, and ye might see his faace
> agaan* [working] *for long enuff. I've knoan folks, village
> lads and lasses, coming over by the old road above which
> runs from Grasmere to Rydal flayt a'most to death there by
> Wishing Gaate to hear the girt voice a groanin' and
> mutterin' and thunderin' of a still evening. Ane he had a
> way of standin' quite still by the rock there in t'path under
> Rydal, and folks could hear sounds like a wild beast coming
> from the rocks, and childer were scared fit to be dead a'most
> . . . He was a gäy good walker, and for a' he had latterly a
> pony and phaeton, I never once seed him in a conveyance in
> whole of my time. But he was never a mountain man. He
> wud gae a deal by Pelter-bridge and round by Red Bank,
> but he was most ter'ble fond of under Nab, and by old high
> road to Swan Inn and back, and very often came as far as
> Dungeon Ghyll. You've happen heerd tell of Dungeon
> Ghyll; it was a vara favourite spot o' Wudsworth's now,
> was that, and he onst made some potry*[4] *about a lamb as fell
> over. And I dar say it was true enuff o' but the rhymes, and
> ye kna they was put in to help it out . . .'*
>   '*Did you ever see Mr. Wordsworth out walking-round
> Pelter-bridge way?'*
>   '*Ay, ay, scores and scores o' times. But he was a lonely
> man, fond o' goin' out wit' his family, and saying nowt to*

noan of 'em. When a man goes in a family way he keeps togither wit' 'em, but many's a time I've seed him a takin' his family out in a string, and niver geein' the deariest bit of notice to 'em; standin' by hissel' and stoppin' behind agapin', wi' his jaws workin' the whoal time; but niver no crackin' wi' 'em, nor no pleasure in 'em, —a desolate-minded man, ya kna. Queer thing that, mun, but it was his hobby, ye kna. It was potry as did it. We all have our hobbies— some for huntin', some cardin' [card-playing], *some fishin', some wrestlin'. He niver followed nowt nobbut a bit o' skating, happen. Eh, he was fond of going on in danger times; —he was always first on the Rydal, however; but his hobby, ye mun kna was potry. It was a queer thing, but it would like enough cause him to be desolate; and I'se often thowt that his brain was that fu' of sic stuff, that he was forced to be always at it whether or no, wet or fair, mumbling to hissel' along the roads.'*

'Do you think,' I asked, 'that he had any friends among the shepherds?'

'Naay, naay, he cared nowt about folk, nor sheep, nor dogs (he had a girt fine one, weighed nine stone, to guard the house), not no more than he did about claes he had on— his hobby was potry'.

'How did he generally dress?'

'Well, in my time then swaller-lappeted ones were i' vogue, but he kep' to all-round plain stuff, and I remember had a cap wi' a neb [peak] to it. He wore that most days'.

'Did you ever read his poetry, or see any books about in the farmhouses?' I asked.

'Ay, ay, time or two. But ya're weel aware there's potry and potry. There's potry wi' a li'le bit pleasant in it, and potry sic as a man can laugh at or the childer understand, and some as takes a deal of mastery to make out what's said, and a deal of Wudsworth's was this sort, ye kna. You could tell fra the man's faace his potry would niver have no laugh in it. His potry was quite different work from li'le Hartley. Hartley 'ud goa running along beside o' the brooks and mak his, and goa in the first oppen door and write what he had got upo' paper. But Wudsworth's potry was real hard stuff, and bided a deal of makking, and he'd keep it in his head for long enough. Eh, but it's queer, mon, different ways volks hes of making potry now. Folks goes a deal to see

*where he's interred; but for my part I'd walk twice distance
over Fells to see where Hartley lies. Not but what Mr.
Wudsworth didn't stand very high, and was a well-spoken
man enough, but quite one to himself . . .'*[5]

He clearly saw himself as a man with a vocation, a mission to
perform and his life, and inevitably that of most of those who
came into close contact with him, was devoted to carrying this
mission through to a successful conclusion.

2

William Wordsworth was born at Cockermouth, in
Cumberland, on 7th April, 1770 and his early boyhood was spent
both there and in Penrith with his mother's parents. His mother
died when he was eight and he remembered little of her although
he presents a highly idealized portrait in *The Prelude*. He recalls
also how '*an intimate friend of hers . . . told me that she once said to
her, that the only one of her five children about whose future life she
was anxious, was William; and he, she said, would be remarkable
either for good or evil*'. This apparently was because of a quick
moody temper rather than because of any early sign of genius
that she had spotted in him. His own memories give a good
example of this:

View of Wordsworth's birthplace at Cockermouth with the River Derwent in
the foreground (Esmor Jones)

> *While I was at my grandfather's house at Penrith, along with my eldest brother Richard, we were whipping tops together in the large drawing-room ... The walls were hung round with family pictures, and I said to my brother, 'Dare you strike your whip through that old lady's petticoat?' He replied, 'No, I won't.' 'Then,' I said, 'here goes'; and I struck my lash through her hooped petticoat, for which no doubt, though I have forgotten it, I was properly punished.*

(Even in so minor a story as this, we notice the dogged egotism, bordering upon irresponsibility, and the tendency to forget the less attractive outcomes which were typical of him.)

That part of his early childhood which was passed at Cockermouth was spent very happily. The River Derwent, which was always to be an influence upon him, ran at the foot of the garden and he bathed in it the summer long. As it flowed, the sound of the river made:

> *ceaseless music that composed my thoughts*
> *To more than infant softness, giving me*
> *Amid the fretful dwellings of mankind*
> *A foretaste, a dim earnest, of the calm*
> *That Nature breathes among the hills and groves.*[6]

Thus, he concludes:

> *Fair seed-time had my soul, and I grew up*
> *Fostered alike by beauty and by fear:*
> *Much favoured in my birth-place, and no less*
> *In that beloved Vale to which erelong*
> *We were transplanted;*[7]

'That beloved Vale' surrounded the Hawkeshead Grammar School to which William was sent with his brother Richard and where he boarded with Anne Tyson in nearby Colthouse from 1779. Much of the early, rather wild, exhilaration in Nature that is described in the earlier part of *The Prelude* was experienced during those schooldays and, along with the experience of Nature, went a growing experience of books:

> *I was left at liberty ... to read whatever books I liked. For example, I read all Fielding's works,* Don Quixote, Gil Blas *and any part of Swift that I liked;* Gulliver's Travels, *and* The Tale of a Tub *being both much to my taste.*

It was here also that he first began to write poetry:

> *The first verses which I wrote were a task imposed by my*
> *master; the subject, 'The Summer Vacation'; and of my*
> *own accord I added others upon 'Return to School'.*

Later, another task produced verses which were '*much*
admired' and '*put it into my head to compose verses from the impule*
of my own mind, and I wrote, while yet a schoolboy, a long poem
running upon my own adventures, and the scenery of the country in
which I was brought up'. Already it seems the germ of *The Prelude*
was with him, although of this poem only the last part survived
and was printed at the beginning of his Collected Works as *Dear*
Native Regions.

During this time at school he was, of course, separated from
his sister, Dorothy, '*the blessing of my later years*', who had been
sent to live with relations near Halifax, and it was not until his
second vacation from Cambridge that the brother and sister came
close together again.

In 1788 Wordsworth went to St. John's College, Cambridge
where he could see from his room the antechapel where stood the
statue of Newton who was, at that time, one of his heroes:

> *The marble index of a mind for ever*
> *Voyaging through strange seas of Thought, alone.*[8]

In spite of the devotion of Book III of *The Prelude* to his
'Residence at Cambridge' it does not seem to have made much
real impression on him although he appears to have thrown
himself wholeheartedly into the social life of the university:

> *Companionships,*
> *Friendships, acquaintances, were welcome all.*
> *We sauntered, played or rioted; we talked*
> *Unprofitable talk at morning hours;*
> *Drifted about along the streets and walks,*
> *Read lazily in trivial books, went forth*
> *To gallop through the country in blind zeal*
> *Of senseless horsemanship, or on the breast*
> *Of Cam sailed boisterously, and let the stars*
> *Come forth, perhaps without one quiet thought.*[9]

But during these years his education developed also in other
respects which were to be of lasting significance so far as he was
concerned.

In the summer of 1788 he underwent the experience that led to his becoming *'a dedicated spirit'* and at the same time came to recognize that his vocation would not be to celebrate Nature alone but also humanity, the simple people of his home countryside. In his first considerable, though highly conventional poem, *An Evening Walk*, which he dedicated to Dorothy, his *'dearest friend'*, he writes about Grasmere and Rydal and describes the characteristic occupations of the area. But he also inserts into the poem a passage in which he tells the story of a wandering woman whose husband had been killed in the American War and whose children die of cold and hunger in her arms. The plight of suffering humanity as well as the beauties of Nature are amongst the earliest themes touched on by the Poet.

The French Revolution began in 1789 and Wordsworth went on a walking tour with his friend Robert Jones that took in France, Switzerland and Italy. In spite of the momentous events taking place in Europe at the time, Wordsworth's interest in politics at this stage appears to have been minimal and it was not until his second visit to France in 1791–2 that the real impact of the Revolution begins. On this visit he met the two people who were to have the biggest influence over his life for the next five years, perhaps for the rest of his life in fact. These were Annette Vallon and Michael Beaupuy.

Beaupuy is celebrated in *The Prelude* but Annette Vallon is not mentioned anywhere, except, perhaps, by implication in some of his poems. Her existence was little known to any except his most intimate friends in his lifetime, and it is only within the present century that the story of Wordsworth's association with her has been uncovered. She met Wordsworth in Orleans in 1791 and in December 1792 she bore his illegitimate child, Caroline. She was certainly the one great passion of his life; in his later marriage to Mary Hutchinson there is no indication of any such feeling as he evidenced for Annette at this time, and there is no doubt about his intention of marrying her when he could. But by February 1793 France and England were at war; Annette was in France and Wordsworth in England without any hope of being reunited.

During his stay in France the meeting with Beaupuy was similarly momentous. Wordsworth had become aware of the impact of the Revolution in a France where:

All hearts were open, every tongue was loud
With amity and glee[10]

and Michael Beaupuy undertook his political education at this
time:

> *when we chanced*
> *One day to meet a hunger-bitten girl,*
> *Who crept along fitting her languid gait*
> *Unto a heifer's motion, by a cord*
> *Tied to her arm, and picking thus from the lane*
> *Its sustenance, while the girl with pallid hands*
> *Was busy knitting in a heartless mood*
> *Of solitude, and at the sight my friend*
> *In agitation said, "Tis against* that
> *That we are fighting', I with him believed*
> *Devoutly that a spirit was abroad*
> *Which might not be withstood*[11]

So Wordsworth became a 'Patriot', a committed advocate of the
revolutionary movement, and from now on:

> *my heart was all*
> *Given to the People, and my love was theirs.*[12]

By French standards, Wordsworth was very mild as a
revolutionary but in an England at war with France and with an
Establishment terrified that the movement might spread across
the Channel, his opinions were enough to make him a dangerous
and radical figure. Certainly the political shock of his own
country at war with the place where, for the time being at least, it
seemed that the hope of Europe lay, added another layer of
anguish to the sense of loss that the separation from Annette
entailed and Wordsworth, in early 1793, was in a lonely and
exposed position. Not even Dorothy was available to turn to and,
almost as a kind of consolation, he hastened on with the
publication of his first volumes of poetry, *Descriptive Sketches*
and *An Evening Walk*, both published by the end of February.

At this time the Bishop of Llandaff, a Dr Watson, published a
sermon with an appendix defending the British Constitution
under the title 'Strictures on the French Revolution'. Wordsworth sat down and wrote an open letter to the Bishop over
the signature '*A Republican*' which was an outspoken defence of
the French Revolution and an attack upon all the best established
of British institutions, demanding also votes for all men and an
equal distribution of wealth. The letter has the white-heat of
genuine political passion but Wordsworth, wisely perhaps,

decided not to publish it and it was not printed in his lifetime. A year later he was writing to a close Cambridge friend, William Matthews, with whom he was hoping to collaborate in a monthly magazine to be called *The Philanthropist*. In these letters he makes it clear that his republican sympathies are as strongly held as ever:

> *I solemnly affirm that in no writings of mine will I ever admit of any sentiment which can have the least tendency to induce my readers to suppose that the doctrines which are now enforced by banishment, imprisonment, etc., etc., are other than pregnant with every species of misery. You know perhaps already that I am of that odious class of men called democrats, and of that class I shall ever continue.*

In a later letter he goes even further:

> *I disapprove of monarchical and aristocratical governments, however modified. Hereditary distinctions, and privileged orders of every species, I think must necessarily counteract the progress of human improvement: hence it follows that I am not amongst the admirers of the British Constitution.*

Now politics matters more than the previous central concerns of nature:

> *I begin to wish much to be in town. Cataracts and mountains are good occasional society, but they will not do for constant companions.*

But Wordsworth's mood now was one of bleak pessimism and one to stay with him. The war between Britain and France was to last nearly nine years and it was by then too late for Wordsworth to be reunited with Annette Vallon. The love that had once been between them had cooled in the interval, and the Wordsworth who returned to France in 1802 was very different from the youthful advocate of revolution.

3

Quite apart from his frustrated love affair with Annette and his despair at the British reaction against the Revolution, Wordsworth, in 1794, had no significant means of making a livelihood. He had decided to give up the idea of going into the Church and had also rejected the Law as another possible career.

(*'I have neither strength of mind, purse, or constitution, to engage in that pursuit.'*) However, he had become reunited with his sister Dorothy, something they had been meaning to bring about for some time. They would be little separated in the years that followed. The two of them stayed together in a Keswick farmhouse: '*We please ourselves in calculating from our present expenses for how very small a sum we could live. We find our own food. Our breakfast and supper are of milk, and our dinner chiefly of potatoes, and we drink no tea*'.

However, the following year his fortunes began to change. His friend, Raisley Calvert, whom he had looked after through a fatal illness, left him £900 and he went to London to stay with another Cambridge friend, Basil Montague, through whom he met John Pinney, who allowed him and Dorothy to have a house at Racedown, near Lyme Regis, rent free. Montague also asked them to look after his two-year-old son, for which he was prepared to pay them £50 a year. So the immediate spectre of poverty had passed for the time being.

While the arrangements over Racedown were in hand, Wordsworth had occasion to be in Bristol where he met both Robert Southey and his friend, Samuel Taylor Coleridge, who was to be the next major influence on his life. In fact, it was not long before brother and sister had left Racedown to move to Alfoxden, which was more to their taste as the countryside reminded them of Cumberland, where they were able to be near Coleridge. The pleasant location of Alfoxden House and the care of Dorothy, coupled with the constant companionship of Coleridge, began the work of healing the suffering which Wordsworth had endured so long. What was to be his greatest period of literary creativity had 'now begun.

In the November after the move to Alfoxden the two Wordsworths and Coleridge began a walking tour which was to make literary history. They were to make a circuit of the hills around Watchet and Dulverton and it was hoped that the expenses of the tour could be covered by writing a poem for a magazine. This led to the co-operation of the two poets and the final outcome was *The Ancient Mariner*, although the bulk of that poem was Coleridge's own creation. Wordsworth, perhaps because of his own recent experiences, was much concerned with the theme of guilt and retribution and he suggested the original shooting of the albatross and the persecution of the mariner that followed but he says himself in his *Autobiographical Memoranda*:

'*a few verses were written by me, and some assistance in planning the poem; but our styles agreed so little, that I withdrew from the concern, and he finished it himself.*'

However, *The Ancient Mariner*, with a few other poems by Coleridge, and a good many by Wordsworth himself was published the following year in the first volume of *Lyrical Ballads*. As well as writing these poems during the spring and summer of 1798, Wordsworth was also engaged in writing *The Ruined Cottage* which was to be part of a long philosophical poem entitled *The Recluse—of Views of Nature, Man and Society*. This was a project that was to remain with Wordsworth for the rest of his writing life and was a task that was often begun but never carried through to a conclusion. *The Prelude*, in fact, was originally intended literally as a 'prelude' to this great philosophical work, which he was strongly encouraged to write by Coleridge. Coleridge had at one time contemplated writing such a major philosophical poem himself but he decided that Wordsworth was better equipped to undertake such a task and he continuously urged him to set about the expression of a system of philosophy in verse, but it was a task for which Wordsworth was by no means equipped either in intellect or temperament. He was always at his best in close observation and the recording of what he observed—as his later work, especially *The Excursion*, demonstrates clearly, philosophy in poetry was never his strong point.

Most of the *Lyrical Ballads* were written at Alfoxden in the middle of 1798 and Dorothy kept a diary of the events of the year which often throws light upon her brother's methods of composition. However, the rather odd behaviour of the three strangers aroused the suspicion of their country Dorset neighbours, especially with a real threat of invasion from France growing all the time. Dorothy, who had a foreign gypsy-like appearance, was a particular cause for concern and the gossip about them was not unlike that which was experienced in similar circumstances by D. H. Lawrence and his wife Frieda in Cornwall during the First World War. In consequence, the owner refused to lease the house to them again the following year and the Alfoxden period came to a compulsory end.

The impending loss of their home made the Wordsworths decide to go on a projected visit to Germany with Coleridge to learn the language; the only problem was that they had no money to cover the expenses. However, *The Ancient Mariner* and the shorter poems that Wordsworth had been working on were enough to make a volume and Cottle of Bristol agreed to publish them anonymously under the title *Lyrical Ballads* and to let them have an advance of ten guineas against publication. This first major work was therefore prepared for the press because Wordsworth needed the money, a principle that he stuck to throughout his life. As well as being self-conscious about his role as a Poet, he was also hard-headed about the professional side of poetry and he was always able to drive a hard bargain with his publishers over the terms that they were to offer him. Meanwhile, as the poems were being prepared finally for printing, Wordsworth and Dorothy went on a walking tour of the Wye valley and this led to a return visit to Tintern Abbey and to Wordsworth's poem on the subject, which became the final poem in *Lyrical Ballads.* It opened with Coleridge's *Ancient Mariner.* When the volume came out in September 1798, it was accompanied by a short Advertisement by Wordsworth which was to launch a new conception of poetry based upon trying to see '*how far the language of conversation in the middle and lower classes of society is adapted to the purposes of poetic pleasure*'. Thus was begun the debate over 'poetic diction' which will be dealt with in detail later. (See Chapter 8.)

The projected visit to Germany took place and while there Wordsworth wrote a number of poems, most notably *Nutting*, the *Lucy* poems and the beginning of *The Prelude*, the intended introduction to the long philosophical poem, *The Recluse.*

Of these *Nutting* is especially interesting as it marks a shift in Wordsworth's view of Nature which was to inform much of his later work. The poem tells of how, as a boy, he left his cottage to go on a nutting expedition. He makes his way violently enough through the countryside until he comes upon his quarry and the poem contrasts his own desire to strip Nature with its own quiet and perfect beauty:

> *O'er pathless rocks,*
> *Through beds of matted fern, and tangled thickets,*
> *Forcing my way, I came to one dear nook*
> *Unvisited, where not a broken bough*
> *Drooped with its withered leaves, ungracious sign*
> *Of devastation; but the hazels rose*
> *Tall and erect, with tempting clusters hung,*
> *A virgin scene!* [13]

For a while he gazes upon the peace and beauty of the scene but
then he seizes upon it:

> Then up I rose,
> And dragged to earth both branch and bough, with crash
> And merciless ravage: and the shady nook
> Of hazels, and the green and mossy bower,
> Deformed and sullied, patiently gave up
> Their quiet being[14]

But, already, as soon as this rape upon Nature had been carried
out, he begins to be aware of what he has done. Nature herself
with quietness and solitude rebukes him:

> Ere from the mutilated bower I turned
> Exulting, rich beyond the wealth of kings,
> I felt a sense of pain when I beheld
> The silent trees, and saw the intruding sky.[15]

Already he is beginning to have those awarenesses that will lead
to such well-known passages as the stolen boat in *The Prelude*,
and the poem ends:

> with gentle hand
> Touch—for there is a spirit in the woods.[16]

It was undoubtedly the influence of Dorothy that led him to this
realization and the time spent with her after the writing of
Lyrical Ballads essentially changed the direction of his poetry.

4

On his return to England, Wordsworth and his sister
stayed with the Hutchinsons and William met again Mary
Hutchinson whom he had known when they were schoolchildren
together in Penrith. He also wrote the second book of *The Prelude*
so that at this time his thoughts must have been very much
running on his early years and the experiences that he had then
had. He and Coleridge went on one of their usual walking tours
and this led them to Grasmere. Later Wordsworth wrote to
Dorothy: '*Coleridge was much struck with Grasmere and its
neighbourhood... There is a small house at Grasmere empty, which,
perhaps, we may take; but of this we will speak*'. The 'small house'
was Town End, as it was then known (now famous as Dove
Cottage) and it was to become the Wordsworths' home for about

Dove Cottage (Esmor Jones)

eight years. It was a pleasant, though small, house and Coleridge and his wife and son soon came to live nearby.

At Grasmere, too, Dorothy kept a journal which is an invaluable source of information about the trio at this stage of their lives. A great number of the poems that Wordsworth wrote at this time related to chance experiences in the neighbourhood or events in his own family life, as when he wrote *The Firgrove* about his brother John's visit to Grasmere in 1800. Here at last he also began work on *The Recluse* but the poem, the first part of which he entitled *Home at Grasmere*, got no further than about 800 lines. These were later incorporated into the opening passages of *The Excursion*, itself to be the concluding section of the long poem beginning with *The Prelude*, which, it was intended, would have the never-to-be-written *Recluse* as its major central section.

However, more immediately urgent was the preparation of a second edition of *Lyrical Ballads* which was published in two volumes in 1800 with a Preface that was a much enlarged version of the Advertisement in the first edition. (This will be considered in detail in Chapter 5.) The first volume included only one new poem by Coleridge, *Love*; after some discussion, *Christabel* was rejected as being too long for the purpose and out of key with the rest of the volume. *The Ancient Mariner* was now placed at the end of the book and Wordsworth merely spoke of '*the assistance of a friend*', in supplying it and three other poems. The second volume consisted entirely of poems by Wordsworth himself and ended with *Michael*. It has been suggested that Wordsworth was less than generous in his treatment of Coleridge in this second edition but the other poet was by now ill, estranged from his wife, and already beginning to rely upon drugs to kill his physical and psychological pain.

Meanwhile there had been further visits from Mary Hutchinson and it seemed likely that she and Wordsworth would be married before long. There was still the unfortunate incident of Annette Vallon across the Channel to be disposed of however. The war with France was still in progress but the odd letter from her still reached the Wordsworths. In 1801 peace was agreed and it was possible to cross the Channel once again. Almost immediately, Wordsworth wrote to Annette and arranged to go to see her and his daughter Caroline, now nine years old, accompanied by his sister. In the months between, Wordsworth wrote a number of important poems such as the *Immortality Ode* and *Resolution and Independence* and it may have been that the coming end to such long unfinished business allowed him to concentrate upon composition once again. Just before they left England for the visit to France, the third edition of *Lyrical Ballads* was published, virtually unchanged except for an expanded Preface by Wordsworth.

The completion of the break with Annette, whom he had clearly ceased to love, took all of a month and we may wonder why it should have been so lengthy a business. In his book on Wordsworth, Herbert Reed makes a good deal of this incident and suggests that it was a turning point in Wordsworth's life. '*His peace of mind, the harmony of his whole life, now depended on a separation from this vivacious, empty Frenchwoman of thirty-six. The dignity of his wordly existence (and Wordsworth had a very grand idea of his own dignity) would be hopelessly compromised if he returned to England with a French wife and a daughter already ten years old*'.[17]

Other changes had also taken place. France was now far removed from the spirit of Revolution that had been such an attractive force ten or so years previously. Wordsworth now hated what he saw as the tyranny of the new Napoleonic regime. The bright hopes of freedom had been dulled.

> *I grieved for Buonaparté, with a vain*
> *And an unthinking grief. The tenderest mood*

Of that Man's mind—what can it be? what food
Fed his first hopes? what knowledge could he *gain?*
'Tis not in battles that from youth we train
The Governor who must be wise and good,
And temper with the sternness of the brain
Thoughts motherly, and meek as womanhood.
Wisdom doth live with children round her knees:
Books, leisure, perfect freedom, and the talk
Man holds with week-day man in the hourly walk
Of the mind's business: these are the degrees
By which true Sway doth mount; this is the stalk
True Power doth grow on; and her rights are these.

Whatever the psychological reasons, there is no doubt that the
Wordsworth who returned from Calais to marry Mary Hutchinson had broken with more than his mistress of ten years back.
From now on he can see nothing good in a France which he feels
has betrayed his own youthful idealism—and perhaps in this
attack upon a once admired country, he is also rationalizing his
own guilty feelings of betrayal now that the break with Annette
was complete. As Reed puts it: '*An uneasy conscience was salved*
with this moral bombast against a nation associated, if only
subconsciously, with the circumstances of his early loss of self-
esteem.'[18]

5

The marriage to Mary Hutchinson was an event that
Dorothy found hard to bear since her exceptional closeness to
her brother would inevitably be challenged by it. Her *Journal*
entry reads:

> *On Monday, October 4th, 1802, my brother William was*
> *married to Mary Hutchinson. I slept a good deal of the*
> *night, and rose fresh and well in the morning. At a little*
> *after eight o'clock, I saw them go down the avenue towards*
> *the church. William had parted from me upstairs. When*
> *they were absent, my dear little Sara prepared the*
> *breakfast. I kept myself as quiet as I could, but when I saw*
> *the two men running up the walk, coming to tell us it was*
> *over, I could stand it no longer, and threw myself on the*
> *bed, where I lay in stillness, neither hearing or seeing*
> *anything till Sara came upstairs to me, and said, 'They are*

coming.' This forced me from the bed where I lay, and I moved, I knew not how, straight forward, faster than my strength could carry me, till I met my beloved William, and fell upon his bosom.[19]

All three, William, Mary and Dorothy, left to return home to Grasmere, and William now had two devoted women to look after him instead of only one. Coleridge, a year later, expressed his misgivings about what this might do to Wordsworth's inspiration and genius as a poet. In a letter he writes: '*I saw him more and more benetted in hypochondriacal Fancies, living wholly amongst* Devotees—*having every the minutest Thing, almost his very eating and drinking, done for him by his Sister, or Wife—and I trembled, lest a Film should rise, and thicken his moral Eye.*' The outcome shows that Coleridge's fears were all too well justified.

By now the Wordsworths were reasonably well-off compared with their earlier financial problems. Just before the visit to

Detail of Mary Wordsworth from a portrait of William and Mary by Margaret Gillies (Reproduced by courtesy of the Trustees of Dove Cottage)

France for the final break with Annette, Lord Lonsdale had paid back an old debt owed to their father and Dorothy and William received about £1,600 each. At Grasmere, first at Town End, and from 1808 at Allan Bank, Wordsworth's five children were born, and two of them later died. Meanwhile in 1805 his very much loved brother John was drowned off Portland Bill and Wordsworth finished the first draft of *The Prelude* although it was to be much revised in the following years. For a matter of two or three years Coleridge was away from the Wordsworths, going to Malta, for the sake of his health and, when he returned, he was much changed from the friend that they had known and loved so much.

The year 1807 saw the publication of *Poems in Two Volumes* which contained, apart from *The Prelude*, most of the poems that Wordsworth had written since the publication of the second edition of *Lyrical Ballads* and this was, on the whole, not well received by the reviewers. In consequence, Wordsworth grew increasingly embittered and resentful. An extract from a letter in which he comments upon one of the more outspoken reviews will give an idea of his state of mind at this time:

> *I am told that there has appeared in the said journal* ['The Critical Review'] *an article purporting to be a review of those poems which is a miserable heap of spiteful nonsense, even worse than anything that has appeared hitherto, in these disgraceful days. I have not seen it, for I am only a chance-reader of reviews, but from what I have heard of the contents of this precious piece, I feel not so much inclined to accuse the author of malice as of sheer, honest insensibility and stupidity.*

The critical debate over the worth of Wordsworth's poetry had begun and continues into our own time, although one ought to add that many of the poems included in *Poems in Two Volumes* are amongst those which his admirers most respect today.

As if this were not enough, he quarrelled with Coleridge in 1810 when a remark of Wordsworth's that Coleridge had '*for years past been an absolute nuisance in the family*' and that he had '*rotted his entrails out*' with drink and drugs was repeated back to him. It is probable that in the context in which they were spoken the words were less offensive than they seem here but Coleridge, not unnaturally, was offended by them and it was not until 1812 that the two were reconciled, though their relationship was never again quite so close *'All outward actions,'* wrote Coleridge in a letter, *'all inward wishes, all thoughts and admirations will be the same—are the same, but—aye, there remains an immedicable* But.' From now onwards the story becomes less important for our purposes. The majority of the poetry which makes Wordsworth's name live for us today was already written, though some still had to be published such as *Peter Bell* and *The Waggoner.* The other major poem to come was, of course, *The Excursion,* published in 1814 and generally attacked by the reviewers. Not even Coleridge could help expressing his disappointment at this colossal failure to write the 'great philosophical poem' that he had always hoped for from Wordsworth. The reviewers accused him of preaching in the poem, 'a tissue of moral and devotional ravings', as one of them put it, and even Crabb Robinson, a faithful friend who had helped to achieve the reconciliation with Coleridge, felt that the poem might draw on Wordsworth 'the imputation of dullness'.

John Keats, who had met Wordsworth with excitement in 1817, wrote in a famous letter of 1818, with reference to *The Excursion*: *'For the sake of a few fine imaginative or domestic passages, are we to be bullied into a certain philosophy engendered in the whims of an egotist? Every man has his speculations, but every man does not brood and peacock over them until he makes a false coinage and deceives himself* ... *We hate poetry that has a palpable design upon us, and, if we do not agree, seems to put its hand into its breeches pocket. Poetry should be great and unobtrusive, a thing which enters into one's soul and does not startle it or amaze it with itself, but with its subject.'* This was the great poem on which Wordsworth had laboured so long and which he had sent to his publisher with high hopes: *'I have at last resolved to send to the press a portion of a poem which, if I live to finish it, I hope future times will "not willingly let die". These you know are the words of my great predecessor* ...' The predecessor referred to was, of course, John Milton, whose shadow continued to dog Wordsworth and from whom he, by now, saw himself in the direct line of poetic descent. We may judge of his disappointment when it was clear that not only hostile reviewers but even his closest friends were embarrassed by the poem and could only compare it unfavourably with 'the former poem', *The Prelude.* Wordsworth's inspiration had gone, although there were many years left of both prosperity and praise. The once outspoken radical, the author of the *Letter to the Bishop of Llandaff* in which he had called

himself 'A Republican', supported the Tory candidate in the
Westmorland Election of 1818 against the outspoken radical
advocate of parliamentary reform, Henry Brougham. Even earlier
he had allowed his hatred for Napoleon to become an
obsession. In 1803 he had joined the volunteers and was drilling
several times a week. In a letter, Dorothy wrote: *'surely there
never was a more determined hater of the French, not one more
willing to do his utmost to destroy them if they really do come.'* In a
pamphlet entitled *Two Addresses to the Freeholders of Westmorland*, he turned his back upon all the radical causes of his youth
and led Shelley to comment: *'What a beastly and pitiful wretch
that Wordsworth! That such a man should be such a poet!'*

But, by now, Wordsworth had obtained more than fame for
his poetry. He had been appointed, in 1813, by Lord Lonsdale as
Distributor of Stamps for Westmorland, an official position that
ensured him a reasonable income for life, and he had moved into
a new and larger home at Rydal Mount. He had become, in
worldly terms, highly successful and a man of property. Not only
was he against parliamentary reform but he also had fears of the
combination of the workers together in the beginnings of the
trades union movement. He defended the massacre of Peterloo
and he had become an Anglican Tory totally opposed to any
change in the established order. Although he continued to write,
and especially to work upon the revisions of *The Prelude*, often to

Rydal Mount where Wordsworth lived from 1813 until his death in 1850
(Esmor Jones)

make its feeling more in keeping with his own later political and religious position, the original inspiration had gone. He received an honorary degree from Oxford University, was awarded a Civil List Pension of £300 a year in 1842, and was appointed Poet Laureate in 1843 on the death of Southey on the assurance that the duties would be very light indeed. The fame and success that his ambitious nature had demanded had come at last but perhaps at a very great price. One remembers Browning's comment upon what the younger poets came to see as his faithlessness:

THE LOST LEADER
Just for a handful of silver he left us,
Just for a riband to stick in his coat —
Found the one gift of which fortune bereft us,
Lost all the others she lets us devote;
They, with the gold to give, doled him out silver,
So much was theirs who so little allowed:
How all our copper had gone for his service!
Rags—were they purple, his heart had been proud!
We that had loved him so, followed him, honoured him,
Lived in his mild and magnificent eye,
Learned his great language, caught his clear accents,
Made him our pattern to live and to die!
Shakespeare was of us, Milton was for us,
Burns, Shelley, were with us—they watch from their graves!
He alone breaks from the van and the freedom,
—He alone sinks to the rear and the slaves!

However, 'the sage of Rydal Mount' lived on until 1850 and, even if the younger generation of poets may have felt that he had let them down he continued to be much respected and loved by friends and neighbours at Grasmere. The house continued to be full of visitors even after Dorothy finally became a victim of mental illness, from which she never recovered, in 1835.

He died in 1850 on 23rd April, the date of Shakespeare's birthday, a coincidence he would have appreciated, and the same year *The Prelude* was finally published. He was buried in Grasmere churchyard in a simple grave alongside which his sister was later to join him. The memorial erected in the church by his friends and neighbours is a final comment upon a complex personality:

Wordsworth's grave in Grasmere churchyard (Esmor Jones)

The memorial tablet erected to the poet by the local villagers (Reproduced by courtesy of the Trustees of Dove Cottage)

TO THE MEMORY OF
WILLIAM WORDSWORTH,
A TRUE PHILOSOPHER AND POET,
WHO, BY THE SPECIAL GIFT AND CALLING OF
ALMIGHTY GOD,
WHETHER HE DISCOURSED ON MAN OR NATURE,
FAILED NOT TO LIFT UP THE HEART
TO HOLY THINGS,
TIRED NOT OF MAINTAINING THE CAUSE
OF THE POOR AND SIMPLE;
AND SO, IN PERILOUS TIMES WAS RAISED UP
TO BE A CHIEF MINISTER,
NOT ONLY OF NOBLEST POESY,
BUT OF HIGH AND SACRED TRUTH

This Memorial
is placed here by his friends and neighbours
in testimony of
Respect, Affection and Gratitude
Anno. MDCCCLI

NOTE: All references to *The Prelude* in this chapter are to the 1850 version. [1]Thomas de Quincey 'William Wordsworth' in *Tait's Edinburgh Magazine*, 1839   [2]William Wordsworth *The Prelude* Bk IV ll 334–7   [3]Hartley Coleridge, son of S. T. Coleridge   [4]*The Idle Shepherd Boys*; or *Dungeon-Ghyll Force*, written in 1800   [5]Quoted in P. Hodgart and T. Redpath *Romantic Perspectives* (Harrap, 1964) pp. 226–8   [6]As 2 Bk I ll 277–81   [7]*ibid*. Bk I ll 301–5   [8]*ibid*. Bk. III ll 62–3   [9]*ibid*. Bk III ll 249–58   [10]*ibid*. Bk VI ll 401–2   [11]*ibid*. Bk IX ll 509–20   [12]*ibid*. Bk IX ll 123–4   [13]William Wordsworth *Nutting* ll 14–21   [14]*ibid*. ll 43–8   [15]*ibid*. ll 50–3   [16]*ibid*. ll 55–6   [17]Herbert Reed *Wordsworth* (Cape, 1930) p. 139   [18]*ibid*. p. 141   [19]Dorothy Wordsworth *Journals* ed. Mary Moorman (O.U.P., 1971)

2

Politics

We have already seen that Wordsworth came under severe criticism from the later Romantic writers for his reversal of his views on the French Revolution and its aftermath and for the increasing conservatism of his later years. Even during his lifetime the real revolutionaries like William Hazlitt, who never lost faith in the Revolution as 'the Good Cause', despised Wordsworth's politics although Hazlitt is generally just in writing about Wordsworth's poetry. Already we begin to feel that we have to discriminate between the man and the poet, and we feel, too, that the Wordsworth of the later period had become self-satisfied and lacking in the fervour of his youth. That there is considerable truth in this seems undeniable and in Chapter I we explored this in terms of his personality and life. In this chapter the intention is to try to explore the same issue but primarily from the point of view of political events and ideas.

The impact of the French Revolution of 1789 upon Europe was so immense that it is easy to forget that it was part of a general series of revolutionary movements of the time. Indeed England might have been seen as preparing the way for this; it had accomplished its own revolution as early as 1688 and had even cut off the head of Charles I in 1649. So when Wordsworth paid the visit to France in 1790 that he describes in Book VI of *The Prelude* he went from a country that had, at least in foreign eyes, successfully accomplished what the French were just beginning to undertake. He found that he and his companion were 'honoured in France' for they bore:

> *the name of Englishmen,*
> *And hospitably did they give us hail,*
> *As their forerunners in a glorious course ;*[1]

To this must also be added the rebellion of England's own colonies in the American uprising and War of Independence of

1775–82—real revolutionary poets like Blake, for example, chronicle vividly the spirit of liberty that seemed to be in the air at the time.

Of Wordsworth's initial delight in this, there is no doubt. France was not alone in her endeavours:

> 'twas a time when Europe was rejoiced,
> France standing on the top of golden hours,
> And human nature seeming born again.[2]

But as Sir Herbert Grierson pointed out in an early, and penetrating, account of Wordsworth and Revolution: 'We know what succeeded, the fierce reaction, the powerful ebb, hatred and mutual suspicion succeeding to amity and glee—September Massacres—the "noyades"—the blood-bath.' A year later Wordsworth was in Paris, a firm believer in the cause of the Revolution itself but sickened by what was happening:

> To Paris I returned. Again I ranged,
> More eagerly than I had done before,
> Through the wide city, and in progress passed
> The prison where the unhappy Monarch lay,
> Associate with his children and his wife
> In bondage ; and the palace, lately stormed
> With a roar of cannon and a numerous host.
> I crossed (a black and empty area then)
> The square of the Carrousel, few weeks back
> Heaped up with dead and dying, upon these
> And other sights looking, as doth a man
> Upon a volume whose contents he knows
> Are memorable, but from him locked up,
> Being written in a tongue he cannot read,
> So that he questions the mute leaves with pain,
> And half upbraids their silence. But that night
> When on my bed I lay, I was most moved
> And felt most deeply in what world I was ...
> I thought of those September massacres,
> Divided from me by a little month,
> And felt and touched them, a substantial dread.[3]

Earlier in *The Prelude*, Wordsworth has told us that he had become a 'Patriot'. However, there seems little doubt that his sympathies lay with the more moderate Girondin party and the passage just quoted makes clear his growing foreboding about the effects of the developing power of the more radical Jacobins, led by Robespierre, who were responsible for the September Massacres and the eventual execution of the king. The cause of the people and the cause of Robespierre were not seen by him to be the same thing at all. Even as late as 1821, he was defending his consistency of position throughout in respect of the Revolution itself:

> *You have been deluded by places and persons, while I have stuck to principles. I abandoned France and her rulers when they abandoned Liberty, gave themselves up to tyranny, and endeavoured to enslave the world.*

The trauma that Wordsworth underwent in seeing the growing destruction of the libertarian idealism with which the Revolution had begun, was one that he shared with many of his contemporaries. But, even in the early stages of the war between France and England that began in 1793, he remained loyal to the French cause in spite of the bitter personal conflict that this meant for him:

> *I rejoiced,*
> *Yea, afterwards—truth most painful to record!—*
> *Exulted in the triumph of my soul,*
> *When Englishmen by thousands were o'erthrown,*
> *Left without glory on the field, or driven,*
> *Brave hearts! to shameful flight.*[4]

To this period also belongs the *Letter to the Bishop of Llandaff*, the most fervent statement of Wordsworth's Republican principles of the time.

But worse was yet in store. The Girondins were completely defeated and largely executed by the Jacobins and, in spite of the death of Robespierre in July 1794, things showed no improvement. As the French turned to wars of aggression instead of self-defence, Wordsworth began to lose his faith in what he was seeing but still struggled to hold on to his old idealistic beliefs:

> *And now, become oppressors in their turn,*
> *Frenchmen had changed a war of self-defence*
> *For one of conquest, losing sight of all*
> *Which they had struggled for: and mounted up,*
> *Openly in the view of earth and heaven,*
> *The seale of liberty . . .*

> *but, roused up, I stuck*
> *More firmly to old tenets, and, to prove*
> *Their temper, strained them more ; and thus, in heat*
> *Of contest, did opinions every day*
> *Grow into consequence, till round my mind*
> *They clung, as if they were the life of it.*[5]

Gradually, especially after the rise to power and triumphant victories of Napoleon, Wordsworth became hardened in his bitterness and anger not only against what had happened in France but also against the English radicals and the Whig Party that could still regard Napoleon, the tyrant of Europe as Wordsworth had come to see him, with approval. The series of poems that he himself classified as *Poems Dedicated to National Liberty and Independence*, mark his conversion to the support of the Tory Party, but they have to be seen in the context of one of the earliest, and most bitter, poems in the sequence when he is observing, in 1802, those flocking to pay tribute to the newly crowned King of France, Napoleon I:

> *Is it a reed that's shaken by the wind,*
> *Or what is it that ye go forth to see?*
> *Lords, lawyers, statesmen, squires of low degree,*
> *Men known, and men unknown, sick, lame, and blind,*
> *Post forward all, like creatures of one kind,*
> *With first-fruit offerings crowd to bend the knee*
> *In France, before the new-born Majesty.*
> *'Tis ever thus. Ye men of prostrate mind,*
> *A seemly reverence may be paid to power ;*
> *But that's a loyal virtue, never sown*
> *In haste, nor springing with a transient shower :*
> *When truth, when sense, when liberty were flown,*
> *What hardship had it been to wait an hour?*
> *Shame on you, feeble Heads, to slavery prone!*

With the sight of '*a Pope...summoned in to crown an Emperor*', France had become a '*...dog returning to his vomit*' and the great hopes that moderate-minded radicals like Wordsworth and Coleridge had once were dashed for ever. The disillusion was complete.

It may be true that for personal reasons of advancement there was some convenience to Wordsworth in embracing the Tory cause at this time, and his increasing bitterness at the way that the Revolution had ended may have had an element in it of rationalization of what it was politically convenient to do. But it is perhaps too easy for the later generation of Romantics to condemn him for his apostacy; to have lived through the experience and to have seen all that one has hoped for destroyed must have produced a bitterness that killed the revolutionary fervour for all time. Certainly those parts of *The Prelude* which deal with this period impress one as a sensitive and committed account of the history of the period and the anguish, almost breakdown, that it brought to the poet. And, of course, Wordsworth was not alone in his reaction to events in France and Europe; many of those who had welcomed the Revolution in its earlier days were increasingly sickened by what it became and turned away from it. It is a not unfamiliar story: much the same might be said of the progress of the Russian Revolution in the twentieth century.

2

Two important political thinkers need to be considered in relation to Wordsworth's shift of position respecting the French Revolution. They are William Godwin, who published his *Political Justice* in 1793, and Edmund Burke who published his *Reflections on the French Revolution* in 1790. In a sense, these two writers stand at opposite ends of a spectrum of much later thinking about political ideas: Godwin is the foundation for much in the radical-anarchist tradition; Burke is the founder of modern Toryism.

Godwin had begun his career as a nonconformist minister but developed views of an atheistic and radical nature. He came to believe that men acted on a basis of reason and that if something could be demonstrated on a rational basis it was impossible not to accept it. Men ought to learn through rational argument to live together in a just and perfect society; it was laws and institutions that made men evil—to remove these was the first step towards the perfect society that Reason alone could bring about. His thinking was especially important in its influence upon the generation of Romantics that followed Wordsworth: his daughter, Mary, became the wife of Shelley, and his second wife's daughter was a mistress of Lord Byron. The philosophical anarchism at the centre of Shelley's thought owed a direct debt to Godwin's work and to *Political Justice* in particular.

Godwin took an essentially idealistic view of human nature and its potential and in the grim period just before the death of Robespierre, the period of the *Letter to the Bishop of Llandaff*, when Wordsworth was most fervently trying to cling to his belief in the Revolution, it was Godwin who was a particular inspiration. Indeed, Basil Willey sees this as '*the vital transition of his* [Wordsworth's] *life, when after his early attachments to France and Godwin he came to share Burke's evaluation and to regard the Revolution as made by man, not evolved by "Nature"'*. Nature had turned, in fact, from '*a revolutionary into a conservative principle*'.[6] Willey convincingly demonstrates the debt that the thought and phrasing of the *Letter to the Bishop of Llandaff* owe to *Political Justice*, especially the willingness to blame all wickedness upon institutions and to see the 'people' as being the source of true righteousness, if left free to exercise rational judgment. '*Left to the quiet exercise of their own judgement, do you think that the people would have thought it necessary to set fire to the house of the philosophic Priestley?*' Indeed in *The Prelude*, Wordsworth looks back, a little wryly, upon the naïvety of the youth who thought at this time that he had found an answer to the increasing despair with which the development of the Revolution was filling him, in the Godwinian philosophy of reason above all things:

> *the dream*
> *Was flattering to the young ingenious mind,*
> *Pleased with extremes and not the least with that*
> *Which makes the human Reason's naked self*
> *The object of its fervour. What delight!*
> *How glorious! in self-knowledge and self-rule,*
> *To look through all the frailties of the world,*
> *And, with a resolute mastery shaking off*
> *The accidents of nature, time, and place,*
> *That make up the weak being of the past,*
> *Build social freedom on its only basis,*
> *The freedom of the individual mind,*
> *Which, to the blind restraints of general laws*
> *Superior, magisterially adopts*
> *One guide, the light of circumstances, flashed*
> *Upon an independent intellect.*[7]

Letters written by Wordsworth in 1794, further echo Godwin's language and disbelief in institutions:

*The enlightened friend of mankind ... should diffuse by
every method a knowledge of those rules of political justice
from which the further any government deviates the more
effectually must it defeat the object for which government
was ordained ... You know perhaps already that I am of
that odious class of men called democrats, and of that class I
shall for ever continue ... I disapprove of monarchical and
aristocratic governments, however modified. Hereditary
distinctions and privileged orders of every species I think
must necessarily counteract the progress of human improvement: hence it follows that I am not amongst the admirers
of the British Constitution.*

Willey demonstrates that, by the time of *Lyrical Ballads*,
Wordsworth was rewriting poems written in draft form earlier, in
order to omit or soften down the 'Godwinian' elements that they
contained and he sees Wordsworth as being under the dominance
of the full Godwin philosophy for only about six months in early
1795, but there can be no doubt of the importance of those six
months in the general development of the poet's thought. What
may have happened is that the attempt to find a basis in
rationality for his political beliefs, as events overtook his wishes
in practice, was a substitution of an abstract ideal for what was
actually taking place. For a time it had seemed, in the French
Revolution, that Nature was becoming realized in the public
events of the day; now that was proving to be no longer true, he
took refuge for a time in a world of abstraction and idealism — he
even tells us in *The Prelude* that he turned to mathematics as an
outlet at this period. But this new faith (if it can be so described)
was short lived and in his play *The Borderers* he seeks to show that
the attempt to live by reason alone is apt '*to produce monsters
rather than supermen*'.[8] Wordsworth's own note of 1842 to the
dramatic poem makes clear its relation to the events of the time
of its composition, 1795–6:

*The study of human nature suggests this awful truth, that,
as in the trials to which life subjects us, sin and crime are
apt to start from their very opposite qualities, so there are
no limits to the hardening of the heart, and the perversion of
the understanding to which they may carry their slaves.
During my long residence in France, while the revolution
was rapidly advancing to its extreme of wickedness, I had
frequent opportunities of being an eye-witness of this process,*

> *and it was while that knowledge was fresh upon my memory that the 'Tragedy of The Borderers' was composed.*

Today *The Borderers* is of little interest to us as one of Wordsworth's works but it represents, nonetheless, the leave-taking of the short flirtation with Godwinism in which he had been engaged.

From now on it was the intuitions that came from Nature in emotional terms, and the philosophy of Burke in intellectual and political terms that were to point the way ahead.

Burke had been a supporter of the rebellion in the American colonies but came to condemn the Revolution in France very roundly, especially in his influential pamphlet *Reflections on the French Revolution*, which he published in 1790. This was a response to a sermon preached towards the end of the previous year by a nonconformist minister, Dr Richard Price, who maintained that the French Revolution was totally justified and that the King of England, similarly, owed his position to the will of the people, who could dismiss him if they decided to do so. Burke argued that the Revolution of 1688 had, in fact, reaffirmed the principle of an inherited monarchy so that the king holds his power as of right not just because the people will it to be so. He champions the doctrine of inherited rights against that of the 'rights of man' which, without any check upon them, will lead to mere brawling and anarchy. In his account of the way the Revolution was going, he foresaw the chaos into which France would fall and the rise of a military dictatorship, such as that offered by Napoleon, to restore order again.

Burke's fundamental principle is of the organic evolution of the state and its institutions rather than violent upheaval and, although he does not approve of the France of before the Revolution, he advocates that there should have been reform from within rather than a wholescale upsurgence that destroys and puts nothing permanent in place of what it has cast down. The National Assembly in revolutionary France was no true parliament but rather a *'profane burlesque of that sacred institute'*. With his new revulsion at what was happening in France, Wordsworth found Burke's theories a considerable support and he, together with Coleridge, became a strong upholder of the principle of the organic evolution of institutions rather than violent change. The *Letter to the Bishop of Llandaff* has been described as an answer to Burke's *Reflections* but by the time that

The scene in the House of Commons if a French invasion were to take place as seen by the satirical cartoonist Gillray (The British Museum)

he comes to revise *The Prelude*, Wordsworth has come to refer to his new mentor with the highest respect:

> *Genius of Burke! ...*
> *I see him, — old, but vigorous in age, —*
> *Stand like an oak whose stag-horn branches start*
> *Out of its leafy brow, the more to awe*
> *The younger brethren of the grove ...*
> *While he forewarns, denounces, launches forth,*
> *Against all systems built on abstract rights,*
> *Keen ridicule; the majesty proclaims*
> *Of Institutes and Laws, hallowed by time;*
> *Declares the vital power of social ties*
> *Endeared by Custom; and with high disdain,*
> *Exploding upstart Theory, insists*
> *Upon the allegiance to which men are born*[9]

It is significant that these lines are not to be found in the earlier 1805 version; they are representative of the later Wordsworth who abandoned the revolutionary aspirations of his youth.

It has been suggested that the central doctrine in Burke is a preference for what has grown rather than for what has been made and that this is what made his attitudes so different towards the American and the French Revolutions. The Americans had grown into an independent people and they were struggling on well-founded principles against a demonstrably unjust rule. The French Revolution was, however, pulling down, with total disregard for tradition, all that had been established in France over the centuries and substituting for natural growth an abstract doctrine of 'reason' which could only lead in the end to chaos.

> *Politics ought to be adjusted, not to human reasonings, but to human nature; of which the reason is but a part, and by no means the greatest part.*
>
> [The revolutionists] *are so taken up with their theories about the rights of man, that they have totally forgotten his nature.*

With statements like these, Burke is rejecting the characteristic belief of the eighteenth century in the light of reason and is maintaining that we have to look at things *as they are*; that no theory is a substitute for practical action in the real situation in which we find ourselves. He is laying the foundations for the philosophy of modern Toryism which aims at a gradual and continuing reform but no sudden break with continuity and tradition or any kind of violent upheaval or revolution. This was the principle upon which Wordsworth came to base his own political views from this time on.

3

The other major political event of Wordsworth's time was an internal one—the Reform Bill of 1832. This was the first in a series of reforms of Parliament that led step-by-step towards changing Britain from an agricultural nation ruled by squires, parsons and wealthy landowners to an industrial nation mainly run by those who controlled industry and commerce. The Bill itself primarily extended the franchise, that is voting rights, although in fact it has been estimated that only about 217,000 extra voters were added to the existing 435,000, an increase of less than 50%. This was because a property qualification was still retained as the basis for appearing on the electoral role;

Britain was still a long way from universal suffrage although the Bill was a step in that direction. Indeed some of the opposition to the Bill was based upon the apparently half-hearted nature of its 'reform'—Coleridge argued that if we were to extend the franchise at all, it was logical to extend it to everyone, even women might conceivably be allowed a vote. Then who could say what kind of mob rule would result! The same people who had watched the excesses of the French Revolution with growing horror felt in many cases that this kind of reform of Parliament was the first step in the same direction here. Predictably enough, by this time Wordsworth was totally opposed to the new proposals.

One of the effects of the Act was to ensure, for the first time, representation of the industrial interests in the large cities such as Manchester, Birmingham and Leeds and in this way to shift the balance from the old landed aristocracy who had dominated Parliament in the past. But it required the inclusion of one's name on an electoral role in order to be able to vote and since there was no secret ballot this led immediately to a much more widespread use of corruption, bribery and intimidation of voters. There was, therefore, some measure of sense in the fears that the reforms would bring about a decline in the standards of public life—although this view could only really be held by those who were secure in the system as it then stood. The 1832 Reform Act was a step on the way to a fuller reform; it could not in itself do more than make a beginning. But it had begun to show where the power actually lay and it now belonged with very different people to those who had held it in the past. David Thomson in his *England in the Nineteenth Century*[10] quotes a leader in *The Times*, published two days after the passing of the Bill, which makes the point very clearly:

Many a green and grizzled jackanapes about the clubs ... was heard to declaim on the 'necessity of placing the "Hero of Waterloo" at the head of affairs', when the 'edge of the sword' would settle the question in a fortnight. We have our own doubts whether the 'Hero of Waterloo' would have resorted to such means, but none at all as to his utter discomfiture had he been hard-hearted or soft-headed enough to try them. But how did the people receive this disgusting language? Did it terrify them into Toryism?—or exasperate them to violence?—or involve them in any course

> *unworthy of respectable and honest citizens? Certainly not.*
> *They shed no blood: they attacked not the person of any*
> *public enemy. They only joined the Political Unions by*
> *myriads—attended meetings by 200,000 at a time—*
> *discussed public questions with more eagerness and ability*
> *than ever—and signed and presented fresh petitions to*
> *Parliament.*

The passing of the Bill demonstrated that it was possible for the British Constitution to reform itself from within without revolution and that such reform was indeed on its way. The very moderate measures introduced in 1832 were the first steps towards a more full-blooded reform of Parliament and changes in the nature of British society to make the country more recognizably like it is today.

But the passage of the Act was the outcome of a long struggle that had been going on between the landed and the manufacturing interests. The plight of the working man, in a time of no organized voice for labour and with high unemployment as a result of the decline in agriculture, was a sorry one. Each man (and in many cases women and children as well) had to take what wages they could and even these tended to be taken back from them by their employers in fines for small offences or by means of such a system as the 'tommy-shop' where workers were forced to buy from their employer goods on account of their wages.

Thomson quotes Disraeli who describes it like this in his novel, *Sybil*, sub-titled *The Two Nations*, published in 1845:

> *The door of Mr Diggs' tommy-shop opened. The rush*
> *was like the advance into the pit of a theatre when the*
> *drama existed; pushing, squeezing, fighting, tearing, shriek-*
> *ing. On a high seat, guarded by rails from all contact, sat*
> *Mr Diggs, senior, with a bland smile on his sanctified*
> *countenance, a pen behind his ear, and recommending his*
> *constrained customers in honeyed tones to be patient and*
> *orderly. Behind the substantial counter, which was an*
> *impregnable fortification, was his popular son, Master*
> *Joseph; a short, ill-favoured cur, with a spirit of vulgar*
> *oppression and malicious mischief stamped on his visage. His*
> *black, greasy lank hair, his pug nose, his coarse red face,*
> *and his projecting tusks, contrasted with the mild and*
> *lengthened countenance of his father, who looked very much*
> *like a wolf in sheep's clothing.*

For the first five minutes Master Joseph did nothing but blaspheme and swear at his customers, occasionally leaning over the counter and cuffing the women in the van or lugging some girl by the hair ...

'Don't make a brawling here,' said Master Joseph, 'or I'll jump over this here counter and knock you down, like nothink. What did you say, woman? are you deaf? what did you say? how much best tea do you want?'

'I don't want any, sire.'

'You never want best tea ; you must take three ounces of best tea, or you shan't have nothing. If you say another word, I'll put you down four. You tall gal, what's your name, you keep back there, or I'll fetch you such a cut as'll keep you at home till next reckoning ... Cuss them ; I'll keep them quiet' : and so he took up a yard measure, and, leaning over the counter hit right and left.

'Oh! you little monster !' exclaimed a woman, 'you have put out my baby's eye.'

There was a murmur ; almost a groan. 'Whose baby's hurt?' asked Master Joseph, in a softened tone.

'Mine, sir,' said an indignant voice ; 'Mary Church.'

'Oh! Mary Church, is it !' said the malicious imp ; 'then I'll put Mary Church down for half a pound of best arrowroot ; that's the finest thing in the world for babbies, and will cure you of bringing your cussed monkeys here, as if you all thought our shop was a hinfant school.'[11]

4

The most famous outbreak of violence was in the summer of 1819 when about 60,000 people gathered in St Peter's Field in Manchester to hear the radical speaker, Hunt. The mounted soldiers who had been sent to arrest the speaker charged the crowd and killed eleven people and injured many others. This was the famous 'massacre of Peterloo' and although the immediate outcome was repression with the passing by the government of the Six Acts designed to prevent public assembly and radical writing, it was clear that reform would have to come if revolution were to be avoided. *The Times* again:

The more attentively we have considered the relations subsisting between the upper and the labouring classes

A view of the 'Peterloo massacre' of 1819 (The Fotomas Index)

> *throughout some of the manufacturing districts, the more painful and unfavourable is the construction which we are forced to put upon the events of last Monday* [i.e. Peterloo]
> *... The two great divisions of society there, are—the masters, who have reduced the rate of wages; and the workmen, who complain of their masters for having done so.*[12]

The road that began with Peterloo led to the Reform Act of 1832.

Wordsworth went so far as to believe that the magistrates and soldiers at Peterloo had some right on their side in charging the crowd. The scars of the terror and the Empire in France had bitten so deeply that he was opposed to all sudden changes in political institutions on a large scale. Still following the doctrine that he had learned from Burke, he argued for gradual and tentative reform. He had no objection to the extension of the franchise to those who lived in the large cities but it should be done in a piecemeal way with slow advances towards reform. In any case, so far as he was concerned, the nature of the reform was very dubious. He remained a strong supporter of the right of Property as the basis of the voting system and was afraid that the extension of the right to vote would change parliamentary representatives into 'mere slavish delegates'. The one-time radical of youth had become a full-blooded reactionary of middle-age.

Yet the best of Wordsworth's early writings, as we shall see in discussion of *Lyrical Ballads*, are well aware of the plight of those working on the land and the results of the decline in the agricultural industry. *The Last of the Flock* is a moving account of a shepherd of the time seeing his flock having to be sold off one by one in order to pay for food for his wife and children. There is no lack of sympathy for *individuals* in his poetry; there is, however, a fundamental failure to understand or sympathize with the economic forces that were leading to far-reaching changes in society. What was taking place was a shift in the economy of the nation from a mainly agricultural to a mainly industrial basis.

Even in the country, things were different from what they had been. Large and rich landlords spent much money on the improvement of their land and the increase of its efficiency but this meant the destruction of the older landed system whereby the labourer could own his own strip of land and use the common land for the grazing of his cattle. The development in the eighteenth century of the enclosures was putting a stop to this. More corn was grown and better stock-breeding resulted but at the cost of the smallholder and the yeoman farmer. A new class of landless labourers was created, wandering around in search of work and either having to accept a small wage and stay in the country or drift into the new towns in the hope of finding work. The world to which Michael, in Wordsworth's poem of that name, had belonged had gone for ever. The towns, too, were undergoing changes. The new methods in industry and the development of machinery meant that people were doing simple and repetitive tasks, often for very low wages; increasing use of machines meant that jobs became scarcer and wages accordingly fell lower still. The industrial working class had begun to come into being and poverty and exploitation of labour were everywhere. Things were not at all helped by the introduction, in 1815, of the Corn Law which was designed to ensure protection against foreign competition for the British farmer and which had the effect of keeping the price of corn artificially high. This led, in turn, to greater poverty on the part of the people who could not afford to buy the other farm products and so to even greater distress in both town and country. To make things even more difficult, the ending of the Napoleonic Wars meant the return to the labour

A Westmorland shepherd (Abbot Hall Art Gallery, Kendal from *Old Photographs of the Lake District*, Hendon Publishing Co. Ltd)

market of a large number of unemployed soldiers just at a time when less labour was needed on the farms.

At this time, before parliamentary reform, the control of the country through parliament was mainly in the hands of the landed classes who used their position to continue the Corn Laws and to protect their own interests. But the real balance of power was shifting and the interests of the industrial magnates gradually began to claim more and more power. In neither case were the interests of the working class, the poor and the dispossessed, being looked after and it was inevitable that the period following the Napoleonic Wars saw the development of organized labour. During the French Revolution itself the fear of the mob had led to the passing of Combination Laws which had made the formation of trades unions illegal, acts of conspiracy. From about 1815 onwards agitation against the Combination Laws became strong amongst the working men and this tended to be supported by the industrial owners who hoped to enlist the workers' support for the abolition of the Corn Laws and parliamentary reform. They assumed that when the workers had gained the right of free collective bargaining with their employers it would prove unnecessary to use that right and the trades union movement would die out. Gradually the unions obtained some rights for themselves and from about 1825 onwards there was a remarkable growth in their numbers although, even as late as 1834, it was possible to sentence the seven Dorchester labourers, the famous 'Tolpuddle martyrs', to transportation for swearing illegal oaths. Disraeli's 'two nations'—the rich and the poor—had come into being in a relatively short time and it was these events that lay in the background of Wordsworth's own lifespan.

As a writer and thinker Wordsworth is able to observe and regret these changes but he can do little to really understand them or to suggest remedies. Fundamentally, his is a conservative philosophy: he notes the passing of the old ways with regret and would like to see them restored again. However, he remains convinced of the power of human dignity and worth to overcome what seems to be leading to destruction on all sides. As he expresses it in one of the most outspoken passages in the 1800 version of the Preface to *Lyrical Ballads*:

> *The human mind is capable of being excited without the application of gross and violent stimulants; and he must have a very faint perception of its beauty and dignity who*

does not know this ... It has therefore appeared to me, that to endeavour to produce or enlarge this capability is one of the best services in which, at any period, a Writer can be engaged; but this service, excellent at all times, is especially so at the present day. For a multitude of causes, unknown to former times are now acting with a combined force to blunt the discriminating powers of the mind, and ... reduce it to a state of almost savage torpor. The most effective of these causes are the great national events which are daily taking place, and the increasing accumulation of men in cities, where the uniformity of their occupations produces a craving for extraordinary incident, which the rapid communication of intelligence hourly gratifies ... When I think upon this degrading thirst after outrageous stimulation, I am almost ashamed to have spoken of the feeble endeavour made in these volumes to counteract it; and, reflecting upon the magnitude of the general evil, I should be oppressed with no dishonourable melancholy, had I not a deep impression of certain inherent and indestructible qualities of the human mind, and likewise of certain powers in the great and permanent objects that act upon it, which are equally inherent and indestructible; and were there not added to this impression a belief, that the time is approaching when the evil will be systematically opposed, by men of greater powers, and with far more distinguished success.

(author's emphasis)

A part, therefore, of the moral purpose of *Lyrical Ballads* is to protest against the changes that are taking place in the traditional way of life.

As a natural conservative, Wordsworth can nonetheless feel a radical anger at the suffering of the individual and it was this that led to his flirtation with the cause of revolution. But, as we have seen, this was soon to turn sour. By contrast, in *Lyrical Ballads*, we see the strength of the old way of life remaining in the qualities of the countrymen that so many of the poems are about, put alongside their present plight and desperation. Throughout his poetical career from *The Female Vagrant*, through the London passages in Book VII of *The Prelude* to *The Excursion*, the changes in society in both the agricultural and industrial way of life are always in the background. *The Excursion*, in particular, which is often regarded as one of Wordsworth's weaker long poems, is,

amongst other things, a poem about the Industrial Revolution.
The Wanderer sees how England has changed in his own time:

> *An inventive Age*
> *Has wrought, if not with speed of magic, yet*
> *To most strange issues. I have lived to mark*
> *A new and unforeseen creation rise*
> *From out the labours of a peaceful Land*
> *Wielding her potent enginery to frame*
> *And to produce, with appetite as keen*
> *As that of war, which rests that night or day,*
> *Industrious to destroy! ...*
>
> *Meanwhile, at social Industry's command,*
> *How quick, how vast an increase! From the germ*
> *Of some poor hamlet, rapidly produced*
> *Here a huge town, continuous and compact,*
> *Hiding the face of earth for leagues—and there,*
> *Where not a habitation stood before,*
> *Abodes of men irregularly massed*
> *Like trees in forests, —spread through spacious tracts,*
> *O'er which the smoke of unremitting fires*
> *Hangs permanent, and plentiful as wreaths*
> *Of vapour glittering in the morning sun.*
> *And, wheresoe'er the traveller turns his steps,*
> *He sees the barren wilderness erased,*
> *Or disappearing; ...*
>
> *When soothing darkness spreads*
> *O'er hill and vale—the Wanderer thus expressed*
> *His recollections—and the punctual stars,*
> *While all things else are gathering to their homes,*
> *Advance, and in the firmament of heaven*
> *Glitter—but undisturbing, undisturbed;*
> *As if their silent company were charged*
> *With peaceful admonitions for the heart*
> *Of all-beholding Man, earth's thoughtful lord;*
> *Then, in full many a region, once like this*
> *The assured domain of calm simplicity*
> *And pensive quiet, and unnatural light*
> *Prepared for never-resting Labour's eyes*
> *Breaks from a many-windowed fabric huge;*

> *And at the appointed hour a bell is heard—*
> *Of harsher import than the curfew-knoll*
> *That spake the Norman Conqueror's stern behest—*
> *A loyal summons to unceasing toil!*
> *Disgorged are now the ministers of day;*
> *And, as they issue from the illumined pile,*
> *A fresh band meets them, at the crowded door—*
> *And in the courts—and where the rumbling stream,*
> *That turns the multitude of dizzy wheels,*
> *Glares, like a troubled spirit, in its bed*
> *Among the rocks below. Men, maidens, youths,*
> *Mother and little children, boys and girls,*
> *Enter, and each the wonted task resumes*
> *Within this temple, where is offered up*
> *To Gain, the master idol of the realm,*
> *Perpetual sacrifice.*[13]

Whatever we may think of the verse, or the political stance, of *The Excursion* as a whole, there can be no mistaking the strength or the anger in these lines. The modern industrialized society dehumanizes; it is essentially a crime against Nature, turning night into day and making slaves of men where they ought to have human dignity and force. Sir Herbert Grierson in his study, *Milton and Wordsworth—Poets and Prophets*,[14] contrasts the response of the two writers to the revolutionary movements of their time and sees Wordsworth as, in the end, coming down on the side of an over optimistic view of human nature. But the echoes in this passage of *Samson Agonistes* are surely very strong; the attack upon the worship of Gain to the exclusion of proper reverence for God and Man and the natural course of things, even in this late work, is as outspoken as the most radical of thinkers could wish. To see him only as a writer whose 'best work' represents '*the rapture of an escape from uncongenial political preoccupations*', as Basil Willey tends to, is to do him an injustice and a disservice. The strength of even the later poetry is the ability to see clearly and honestly the plight of his fellow men and to respond to it. Basically he is seeking a way to lead mankind back to Paradise:

> *all his thoughts now flowing clear,*
> *From a clear fountain flowing, he looks round*
> *And seeks for good; and finds the good he seeks.*

Seen from this angle, we can recognize an awe-inspiring consistency in Wordsworth's work and thought that does not totally justify the attacks, so easily made with hindsight, of his successors who, after all, had less tumultuous times to live through.

[1] William Wordsworth *The Prelude* (1850 version) Bk VI ll 403–5 [2]*ibid.* (1805 version) Bk VI ll 352–4 [3]*ibid.* (1805 version) Bk X ll 39–66 [4]*ibid.* (1805 version) Bk X ll 259–64 [5]*ibid.* (1805 version) Bk X ll 792–805 [6]Basil Willey *The Eighteenth Century Background* (Chatto and Windus, 1940) p. 241 [7] As 1 (1805 version) Bk X ll 815–30 [8] As 6 p. 254 [9] As 1 (1850 version) Bk VII ll 512–30 [10]David Thomson *England in the Nineteenth Century* (Pelican, 1950) pp. 75–6 [11]*ibid.* pp. 38–9 [12]*ibid.* p. 40 [13]William Wordsworth *The Excursion* Bk VIII ll 87–185 [14] Sir Herbert Grierson *Milton and Wordsworth—Poets and Prophets* (Cambridge U.P., 1937)

3

Nature

I

Wordsworth is generally thought of as being a poet concerned, above all, with Nature. What that word meant to him, and the influence that he saw Nature as having had on his life and development as a poet, is a complex question and much of this book is concerned with exploring this through his poetry. Undoubtedly his best known poem is *I wandered lonely as a cloud* (which, as we shall see later, is by no means as simple a poem as it may appear at first sight) and the associations that such a poem has for us may stop us from seeing Wordsworth as man or poet at all clearly. Whatever else he may have been he was certainly no mere dreamer lost in the silent contemplation of the beauties of Nature and out of touch with the real world. The man who could write some of his most powerful verse about the crossing of the Simplon Pass and who could climb Helvellyn when well into his seventies was very different from the view often taken of him by those who think of him in terms of a commonly held view of 'The Daffodils' alone. There is no doubt that Wordsworth came to see himself as having a specially chosen role in which his own response to Nature was of first importance, but he lived at a time when attitudes towards the natural world in general were undergoing important changes and this chapter aims to try to place this in perspective and to examine some of the ideas about Nature held by Wordsworth and his contemporaries.

For most of the eighteenth century, the commonly accepted view of Nature was closely linked with the idea of natural order. It was an age of rationalism and the mathematics and physics of Newton led support to a view that the universe was a huge machine constructed according to certain physical laws which we could now understand; a gigantic clock that had been wound up and was now able to be left very much to its own devices. Nature was the book in which we could read and understand the laws that underpinned this machine-like universe; it was itself neutral and open to our inspection and understanding. Above all, Newton had explored these principles and organized them into a system; little but refinement of our understanding remained to be achieved.

A similar view could be taken of the purposes of the writer and the artist—their main concern was to represent 'general nature' and not to concern themselves with detail and the particular. Dr Johnson, one of the most important writers and theorists of his time, maintains through the words of Imlac in *Rasselas:*

> *The business of a poet ... is to examine, not the individual but the species; to remark general properties and large appearances. He does not number the streaks of the tulip.*

Elsewhere, in his *Preface to Shakespeare*, he writes:

> *Nothing can please many, and please long, but just representations of general nature.*

In the art of gardening the ideal was the formally laid out garden and, at times, this was carried to absurd and excessive lengths. In the same way, both in the visual art and the poetry of the period, human figures in a landscape tend to be vague and generalized portraits, there to help give perspective but not brought home to us as individuals in any sense. Gray's *Elegy*, in its famous opening lines, provides a good example of this:

> *The curfew tolls the knell of parting day,*
> *The lowing herd wind slowly o'er the lea,*
> *The ploughman homeward plods his weary way,*
> *And leaves the world to darkness and to me.*

Contrast this, written in 1742 and published in 1750, with the first stanza from Wordsworth's *The Last of the Flock* in 1798:

> *In distant countries have I been,*
> *And yet I have not often seen*
> *A healthy man, a man full grown,*
> *Weep in the public roads, alone.*
> *But such a one, on English ground,*
> *And in the broad highway, I met;*
> *Along the broad highway he came,*
> *His cheeks with tears were wet:*
> *Sturdy he seemed, though he was sad;*
> *And in his arms a Lamb he had.*

We are immediately in the world of the close-up with an almost obsessive attention to detail; here, and in the rest of the poem, the shepherd is sharply individualized as a real person suffering real pain as he sees his flock of sheep dwindling one by one until the lamb he now carries is all that is left.

This switch in attention from the general to the particular did not come about suddenly and, already in the eighteenth century, alongside the formality and concern with order and generalization which was so fashionable, there were the stirrings of different and more particularized interests.

As early as 1709, for example, Shaftesbury was arguing for more attention to be paid to uncultivated Nature instead of the carefully laid out garden of his time:

> *I shall no longer resist the passion in me for things of a natural kind; where neither* Art, *nor the* Conceit *or* Caprice *of Man has spoiled their genuine* Order ... *Even the rude* Rocks, *the mossy* Caverns, *the irregular unwrought* Grottoes, *and broken Falls of Waters, with all the horrid Graces of the* Wilderness *itself, as representing* NATURE *more, will be the more engaging, and appear with the Magnificence beyond the formal Mockery of princely Gardens.*[1]

Addison in *The Spectator*, No. 414, makes a similar point:

> *There is something more bold and masterly in the rough careless strokes of nature than in the nice touches and embellishments of art. The beauties of the most stately garden or palace lie in a narrow compass, the imagination immediately runs them over, and requires something else to gratify her; but, in the wild fields of nature, the sight wanders up and down without confinement, and is fed with an infinite variety of images ... For my own part, I would rather look upon a tree in all its luxuriance and diffusion of boughs and branches, than when it is thus cut and trimmed into a mathematical figure.*[2]

The debate over how to lay out a garden was an important one and one in which Wordsworth himself was to have an interest. He was a devoted and skilled gardener and gave much thought to the principles on which he would lay out the gardens that he constructed, as we shall see later. But the contrast that is being made here between Nature as it really was, 'rude and unconfined', and Nature as tended and 'improved' by the art and hand of man was a debate that was echoed in the painting and the poetry of the time also. As well as the *Elegy*, Gray could also write a poem like *The Bard* which presents a very different picture of Nature to the country churchyard at Stoke Poges:

> *On a rock, whose haughty brow*
> *Frowns o'er old Conway's foaming flood,*
> *Robed in the sable garb of woe,*
> *With haggard eyes the Poet stood —*
> *Loose his beard and hoary hair*
> *Streamed, like a meteor, to the troubled air —*
> *And with a master's hand, and prophet's fire,*
> *Struck the deep sorrows of his lyre.*[3]

It would therefore be a very great mistake to oversimplify the eighteenth century's attitude towards Nature and the roots from which Wordsworth's own work springs. Throughout the century, and increasingly towards its end, the claims of a Nature that was rugged and wild were being asserted alongside the continuing belief in an ordered and controllable universe.

Central to the discussion was the publication in 1756 of Burke's *A Philosophical Enquiry into the Origin of our Ideas of the Sublime and Beautiful*. He argued here that men were possessed of two fundamental instincts—self-preservation and self-propagation. Any objects perceived by our senses appealed to one or other of these two instincts. Those that were smooth and gentle and pleasing appealed to the instinct of self-propagation and were called 'Beautiful'. Those which filled us with a sense of pain or danger appealed to the sense of self-preservation and were called 'Sublime'. Nonetheless, the dangerous and the frightening could also be enjoyed when we knew that, after all, there was no real danger associated with it. We like, in fact, to feel frightened and enjoy it *'when without danger we are conversant with terrible objects'*. For many of Burke's contemporaries the experience of mountain scenery was possessed of many of the qualities, such as vastness, darkness, solitude and infinity, that he included within his definition of the sublime. Kant writing in his *Critique of Aesthetic Judgement* in 1790 puts it like this:

> *The astonishment amounting to terror, the awe and thrill of*
> *devout feeling, that takes hold of one when gazing upon the*

prospect of mountains ascending to heaven, deep ravines and
torrents raging there, deep-shadowed solitudes that invite
one to melancholy and the like—all these, <u>when we are</u>
<u>assured of our own safety, do not produce actual fear.</u>

(author's emphasis)

Sublimity is, in fact, '*a voluntary experiencing of the fearful, a*
sense of horror made "aesthetic" by a recognition of security'. If we
compare this with Wordsworth's account in *The Prelude* of his
sight of the Alps, in the well-known Simplon Pass passage, we
can see him responding to exactly the same kind of feelings as
have been defined by Burke and Kant:

> *The immeasurable height*
> *Of woods decaying, never to be decayed,*
> *The stationary blasts of waterfalls,*
> *And in the narrow rent at every turn*
> *Winds thwarting winds, bewildered and forlorn,*
> *The torrents shooting from the clear blue sky,*
> *The rocks that muttered close upon our ears,*
> *Black drizzling crags that spake by the way-side*
> *As if a voice were in them the sick sight*
> *And giddy prospect of the raving stream,*
> *The unfettered clouds and region of the Heavens,*
> *Tumult and peace, the darkness and the light—*
> *Were all like the workings of one mind, the features*
> *Of the same face, blossoms upon one tree;*
> *Characters of the great Apocalypse,*
> *The types and symbols of Eternity,*
> *Of first and last and midst and without end.*[4]

Interestingly in this passage Wordsworth is seeking to accom-
modate the wildness of Nature in its untamed mood with a sense
of order and of purpose and design; the contraries, properly
understood, the '*tumult and peace, the darkness and the light*' are
all '*the workings of one mind*'.

This concern to bring together opposites and, in particular, an
interest in the effects of light and shade in mountain scenery has
its roots in earlier development in landscape painting and
especially in the work of artists such as Claude Lorrain and
Salvator Rosa. Claude Lorrain (1600–82) is especially important
because his work was well known to the eighteenth century
English travellers who had begun to discover for themselves the

Simplon Pass (Mary Evans Picture Library)

alpine scenery and because he was enthusiastically collected by Wordsworth's close friend and patron, Sir George Beaumont. Claude's painting was noted for its use of light and its capacity to explore infinite distances while still retaining a central expression of harmony between man and Nature—very much the kind of experience that Wordsworth is exploring in the passage just quoted. Sir Joshua Reynolds speaks of him as combining separate scenes of Nature into one idealized whole; like some of the gardeners of the period he took from Nature but sought also to improve upon it. In one of his *Discourses*, Reynolds writes: '*Claude Lorrain . . . was convinced, that taking nature as he found it seldom produced beauty. His pictures are a composition of the various draughts he had previously made from various beautiful scenes and prospects.*' His importance can be gauged by Constable's recalling that after being shown Claude's painting, *Hagar and the Angel*, by Sir George Beaumont he '*looked back on this exquisite work as an important epoch in his life*'.

Wordsworth's own first published poem, *An Evening Walk*, is in its subject matter and general feel very like a Claude painting:

> *How pleasant, as the sun declines, to view*
> *The spacious landscape change in form and hue!*
> *Here, vanish, as in mist, before a flood*
> *Of bright obscurity, hill, lawn, and wood;*
> *There, objects, by the searching beams betrayed,*
> *Come forth, and here retire in purple shade;*
> *Even the white stems of birch, the cottage white,*
> *Soften their glare before the mellow light;*

Hagar and the Angel by Claude Lorrain (Reproduced by courtesy of the Trustees of the National Gallery, London)

The skiffs, at anchor where with umbrage wide
Yon chestnuts half the latticed boat-house hide,
Shed from their sides, that face the sun's slant beam,
Strong flakes of radiance on the tremulous stream :
Raised by yon travelling flock, a dusty cloud
Mounts from the road, and spreads its moving shroud ;
The shepherd, all involved in wreaths of fire,
Now shows a shadowy speck, and now is lost entire.[5]

This poem, composed in 1793, is almost entirely a conventional eighteenth century poem in its feeling. The landscape is appreciated but its ultimate effect is to reinforce a feeling of security and of peace. The shepherd is introduced as part of the landscape, to give it scale and human interest, but is much more like Gray's ploughman than Wordsworth's later shepherd in *The Last of the Flock*.

If Claude's paintings produced finally a sense of order and harmony, those of Salvator Rosa, especially his wilder scenes of waterfalls, mountains and precipices, come closer to what Burke had been describing in his account of the sublime and at times very close to some of Wordsworth's own description of alpine scenery such as that already quoted. Between them Claude and Rosa prepared many eighteenth century travellers about to make the Grand Tour for what they were going to see and it was almost impossible not to see the scenery, to some extent, through their eyes.

Enthusiasm for their paintings came very much earlier than the first attempts by later eighteenth century poets to convey the same scenes and feelings in verse. James Thomson, one of the foremost of these, has been described as giving us in *The Seasons* (1726–30) 'a gallery of paintings'.[6] Here, for example, is his description of the moon in autumn:

The western sun withdraws the shortened day,
And humid evening, gliding o'er the sky
In her chill progress, to the ground condensed
The vapours throws, Where creeping waters ooze,
Where marshes stagnate, and where rivers wind,
Cluster the rolling fogs, and swim along
The dusky-mantled lawn. Meanwhile the moon
Full-orbed, and breaking through the scattered clouds,
Shews her broad visage in the crimsoned east.
Turned to the sun direct, her spotted disc, . . .

A smaller earth, gives all its blaze again,
Void of its flame, and sheds a softer day.[7]

Between them Claude's sense of light and distance and Rosa's gloom taught a later generation how to look at and appreciate mountain scenery and their paintings are the starting point for an appreciation of Wordsworth's own view of landscape.

2

To the categories of the sublime and the beautiful as defined by Burke, later writers added a third, known as 'the picturesque'. This, too, found an early manifestation in the field of landscape gardening. Designers of gardens such as William Kent used the paintings of the Italian landscape painters as inspirations for their own landscaping in reality. Kent sought to use the principles of perspective and the effects of light and shade, created by winding walks and flowing streams, to produce 'natural pictures' which had a strong resemblance to paintings by Claude Lorrain and Salvator Rosa. The essence of the picturesque, as it evolved, in the fashionable gardening of the time, was to unite together opposites, to create successive scenes which had dramatic contrasts built into them and which could be used to evoke an emotional response. Ruins, cypress trees, grottoes and sunny meadows were all used to create strong effects, and very often gnarled trees and ruined buildings were incorporated into the landscape to create the effect of melancholy and solitude which was very fashionable at the time, often in a rather exaggerated and sentimental kind of way.

What had begun as a taste in gardening rapidly also became one of travel. An early visitor to the Lake District was William Gilpin who wrote his *Tour of the Lakes* in 1789 and set the fashion for the way in which travellers would look at the scenery. Each view was divided into three parts: *Background*, containing mountains and lakes; *Off-skip*, comprising valleys, woods, rivers; *Foreground*, comprising rocks, cascades, broken ground and ruins. The analogies both with painting and with the effects of picturesque landscape gardening are quite clear. It is worth comparing Gilpin's account of Tintern Abbey with that of Wordsworth later: *'Ivy, in masses uncommonly large, has taken possession of many parts of the walls; and gives a happy contrast to the grey-coloured stone ... Nor is this undecorated. Mosses of*

Tintern Abbey (Crown copyright. Reproduced by permission of the Controller of Her Majesty's Stationery Office and the Royal Commission on Ancient and Historical Monuments in Wales)

various hues, with lychens, maiden hair, penny-leaf and other humble plants, overspread the surface . . . all together they give those full-blown tints which add the richest finishing to a ruin.' A whole new language for describing scenes in their picturesque splendour was created: the different views are recommended in the guidebooks to the Lakes in terms of 'stations', positions from which the best views (the ones most like paintings) can be enjoyed.

In order to increase the enjoyment the traveller was recommended to take with him a 'landscape mirror', also known as a Claude Lorrain glass, making its origins and purposes quite clear. We know that Gray took one with him on his own travels in the Lakes and another traveller, Thomas West, explains its use in detail:

> *Where the objects are great and near, it removes them to a due distance, and shows them in the soft colours of nature, and in the most regular perspective the eye can perceive, or science demonstrate.*
> *The mirror is of the greatest use in sunshine; and the person using it ought always to turn his back to the object that he views. It should be suspended by the upper part of the case, holding it a little to the right or left (as the position of the*

The Claude glass (Reproduced by courtesy of the Trustees of the British Museum)

*parts to be viewed require) and the face screened from the
sun.*

*The mirror is a plane-convex glass, and should be the
segment of a large circle; otherwise distant and small objects
are not perceived in it; but if the glass be too flat the
perspective view of great and near objects is less pleasing, as
they are represented too near. These inconveniences may be
provided against by two glasses of different convexity. The
dark glass answers well in sunshine; but on cloudy and
gloomy days the silver foil is better.—Whoever uses
spectacles upon other occasions, must use them in viewing
landscapes in these mirrors.*

The use of the Claude glass to frame the scene and to enable one
to use the optical instrument to discipline and improve on
Nature has clear analogies with landscape painting itself; it also
has something in common with the modern practice of
preserving the impression of a scene by taking a photograph.
With the camera, too, we frame a scene and attend to its
composition; as with the Claude glass, we are able to use filters
(and also kinds and speeds of film) to idealize the scenes that we
want to record.

It is perhaps not too fanciful to see many of Wordsworth's
own poems as something of the equivalent to modern
photography, the capturing of a scene in words as a modern
tourist would seek to capture it in a photograph. The titles of
many sequences of his poems lend support to this view:
Memorials of a Tour on the Continent, 1820, *Memorials of a Tour
in Italy*, 1837, and so on. Very often, although he affected to
scorn the contemporary fashion for the picturesque, the poems
show the same care in *visual* composition as they do in verbal and
his own *Guide to the English Lakes* (1810) was originally published
anonymously as an introduction to Joseph Wilkinson's series of
views of the Lake District printed by Ackermann. Throughout,
it is based clearly on picturesque principles and argues strongly
against the intrusion into the landscape of pillars introduced to
echo the effect of paintings and of new houses which did not
blend with the surroundings. He was *'disgusted with the new
erections and objects about Windermere'* and he fights a ceaseless
battle against the tastelessness of white buildings and houses
being introduced into the district: *'In Nature, pure white is
scarcely ever found but in small objects, such as flowers; or in those*

which are transitory, as the clouds, foam of rivers, and snow . . . an object of pure white can scarcely ever be managed with good effect in landscape-painting.' Earlier, as the stolen boat passage in *The Prelude* records, Wordsworth had learned how fearful Nature could be but he also came to learn that if one were faithful to it, if, in fact, one carried out one's vocation as a poet, Nature was essentially a healing, a comforting, and a beneficent force. The task was, essentially, one of learning to co-operate with the handiwork of God, to '*let Nature be your teacher*' in a literal as well as metaphorical sense.

3

The moment when Wordsworth first became clearly aware of his role as the poet who was to present Nature as she was to the world is quite clearly identified. When he was 73 he told a Miss Fenwick how on the road between Hawkshead and Ambleside he first noticed the darkening boughs and leaves of the oak tree '*fronting the bright west*'. It was a moment which gave him '*extreme pleasure*' and he continued:

> *The moment was important in my poetical history; for I date from then my consciousness of the infinite variety of natural appearances which had been unnoticed by the poets of any age or country, so far as I was acquainted with them; and I made a resolution to supply, to some degree, the deficiency. I could not have been at that time above 14 years of age.*

In Book VIII of *The Prelude (Retrospect)* he recalls these early experiences and the sense of joy and dedication they brought:

> *I remember, far from home*
> *Once having strayed, while yet a very child,*
> *I saw a sight, and with what joy and love!*
> *It was a day of exhalations, spread*
> *Upon the mountains, mists and steam-like fogs*
> *Resounding everywhere, not vehement,*
> *But calm and mild, gentle and beautiful,*
> *With gleams of sunshine on the eyelet spots*
> *And loop-holes of the hills, wherever seen,*
> *Hidden by quiet process, and as soon*
> *Unfolded, to be huddled up again . . .*

> *With delight*
> *As bland almost, one evening I beheld,*
> *And at as early age (the spectacle*
> *Is common, but by me was then first seen)*
> *A shepherd in the bottom of a vale*
> *Towards the centre standing, who with voice,*
> *And hand waved to and fro as need required,*
> *Gave signal to his dog, thus teaching him*
> *To chase along the mazes of steep crags*
> *The flock he could not see . . .*[8]

He records these incidents in his early schoolboy poem, *The Vale of Esthwaite*, and they are similar to the well-known moment returning home after a dance in Book IV in the early morning:

> *Two miles I had to walk along the fields*
> *Before I reached my home. Magnificent*
> *The morning was, a memorable pomp,*
> *More glorious than I ever had beheld.*
> *The sea was laughing at a distance; all*
> *The solid mountains were as bright as clouds,*
> *Grain-tinctured, drenched in empyream light;*
> *And in the meadows and the lower grounds*
> *Was all the sweetness of a common dawn—*
> *Dews, vapours, and the melody of birds,*
> *And labourers going forth into the fields.*
> *Ah! need I say, dear Friend! that to the brim*
> *My heart was full; I made no vows, but vows*
> *Were then made for me; bond unknown to me*
> *Was given, that I should be, else sinning greatly,*
> *A dedicated Spirit. On I walked*
> *In blessedness, which even yet remains.*[9]

But, in Wordsworth, this was not to be any passive acceptance and recalling of the external beauties of Nature. As we have seen, he was essentially a devotee of the picturesque, and fundamental to this was the activity of the human mind in co-operating with Nature to change it into Art. The psychology of the eighteenth century deriving from the thought of Locke and Hartley saw the mind as passive in perception; the mind was like a blank sheet of paper at birth upon which the external world wrote its impressions. The sublime and the beautiful, of which Burke had written, operated *upon* the mind which received the impressions that they imprinted upon it. But the picturesque involved acts of deliberate choice, selection and arrangement; the mind has become a partner with Nature in the forms that it is perceiving.

This is essentially the view of Nature and his understanding of it that Wordsworth presents in so central a poem as *Tintern Abbey*. We have already noted how Gilpin described the sight of Tintern in terms of the picturesque and Wordsworth's own account in his poem is filled with details that recall the picturesque painting: the potential of the sublime is there but it is controlled by images that soften and contain the immensity.

> *Once again*
> *Do I behold these steep and lofty cliffs,*
> *That on a wild secluded scene impress*
> *Thoughts of more deep seclusion; and connect*
> *The landscape with the quiet of the sky.*
> *The day is come when I again repose*
> *Here, under this dark sycamore,* and view*
> *These plots of cottage-ground, these orchard-tufts,*
> *Which at this season, with their unripe fruits,*
> *Are clad in one green hue, and lose themselves*
> *'Mid groves and copses.*[10]

But the thoughts that result from the contemplation of Tintern Abbey do not come unbidden; they are deliberately sought out by the poet:

> *how oft—*
> *In darkness and amid the many shapes*
> *Of joyless daylight; when the fretful stir*
> *Unprofitable, and the fever of the world,*
> *Have hung upon the beatings of my heart—*
> *How oft, in spirit, have I turned to thee,*
> *O sylvan Wye! thou wanderer thro' the woods,*
> *How often has my spirit turned to thee!*[11]

---

* The sycamore tree, in particular, strongly recalls the paintings of Claude and his successors. Sir George Beaumont is said to have asked Constable on one occasion, 'Do you not find it very difficult to determine where to place your brown tree?' Constable replied that he never put such a thing into a picture but Sir George, who carried a brown fiddle around with him when he went on a sketching expedition to stand in for a brown tree, was of the opinion that every good picture ought to include a brown tree as a matter of course.

What is experienced in this act of deliberate turning towards the memory of what has been felt at Tintern Abbey is much more than just the recalling of something that has happened to him in the past; it is an act of re-creation in the present in which the mind of the poet plays an active part:

> *Therefore am I still*
> *A lover of the meadows and the woods,*
> *And mountains; and of all that we behold*
> *From this green earth; of all the mighty world*
> *Of eye, and ear, —both what they half create,*
> *And what perceive; well pleased to recognise*
> *In nature and the language of the sense*
> *The anchor of my purest thoughts, the nurse,*
> *The guide, the guardian of my heart, and soul*
> *Of all my moral being.*[12]

(author's emphasis)

As his thoughts turn to the 'sylvan Wye' its influence is clearly seen:

> *To them I may have owed another gift,*
> *Of aspect more sublime; that blessed mood,*
> *In which the burthen of the mystery,*
> *In which the heavy and the weary weight*
> *Of all this unintelligible world,*
> *Is lightened:—that serene and blessèd mood,*
> *In which the affections gently lead us on, —*
> *Until, the breath of this corporeal frame*
> *And even the motion of our human blood*
> *Almost suspended, we are laid asleep*
> *In body, and become a living soul:*
> *While with an eye made quiet by the power*
> *Of harmony, and the deep power of joy,*
> *We see into the life of things.*[13]

Upon our reading of this paragraph of verse will depend much of our response to Wordsworth. It can easily be dismissed as mere phrase-making, the use of a facility in versifying which convinces (almost lulls us into unconsciousness as we read it) but by a kind of poetic sleight-of-hand. We are caught in the music of the verse to such an extent that we fail to attend to the words; if we do and ask what Wordsworth is actually saying we find it very difficult to tie it down to any kind of precision. But to read it like this is to do so with precisely the lack of that attention which the poetry here, as elsewhere in Wordsworth, demands of us. Of course he is not saying that the Wye and the scenery that surrounds it is itself the source of the knowledge that he claims, the ability to *see into the heart of things*. This is essentially the product of the poet's own mind, the recollection of the 'beauteous forms' of the Wye valley creates in him a mood that, in turn, *leads* to thought and insight. The ordered natural world that the *recollection* of the Wye valley presents is an indication of an ordered world in the life of man also and a similar harmony and order can be glimpsed in the universe to that which the imagination of the poet perceives in the natural world that he is remembering. The importance of this cannot be over-stated: constantly Wordsworth writes of a remembered Nature, one seen in reflective, in 'pensive mood'; but it is a Nature ordered by the art of landscape, by the operation of the human imagination, by Art, by the work of the poet, in fact, that is the source of the tranquil restoration. This is the element of the picturesque that is central to all his work.

4

In his insistence upon the creative and imaginative act of the mind of man, Wordsworth is coming very close to the idea of the Imagination as defined by Coleridge although he seems to have developed his own thinking independently before meeting Coleridge. Certainly while he was at Cambridge he had begun to recognize the synthesizing power of the human imagination:

> To every natural form, rock, fruit or flower,
> Even the loose stones that cover the highway,
> I gave a moral life, I saw them feel,
> Or link'd them to some feeling: the great mass
> Lay bedded in a quickening soul ...[14]

It would be a mistake to see this as purely an emotional response to Nature in Wordsworth; for him this apprehension of the unity in all things was an act of the intellect and the imagination; the human mind was active in its perception—as the landscape painter co-operated with Nature to produce a work of art that was itself a comment upon the natural scene with which he began so the poet, too, is engaged in a similar activity of the discovery of the ordered pattern in all things. The discovery is one that is essentially part of the same process that had led Newton to discover an order in the physical universe. To discern the laws of our moral and psychological universe is the next great task and it is one to which the poet is called. The attempt to carry it out is the essential subject-matter of *The Prelude*:

> *The mind of man is framed even like the breath*
> *And harmony of music; there is a dark*
> *Invisible workmanship that reconciles*
> *Discordant elements, and makes them move*
> *In one society ...*
> *I believe*
> *That Nature, oftentimes, when she would frame*
> *A favoured being, from his earliest dawn*
> *Of infancy doth open out the clouds,*
> *As at the touch of lightning, seeking him*
> *With gentlest visitation; not the less,*
> *Though haply aiming at the self-same end,*
> *Does it delight her sometimes to employ*
> *Severer interventions, ministry*
> *More palpable, and so she dealt with me.*[15]

It has been suggested, notably by Basil Willey in *The Eighteenth Century Background*,[16] that, as Wordsworth's political views changed, partly at least as a consequence of what he saw happening in France, his attitude towards Nature changed also. He himself had written: '*Cataracts and mountains are good occasional society, but they will not do for constant companions*' and Willey suggests that '*his later life perhaps proved the truth of this statement.*' It is certainly true that as Wordsworth settled more comfortably and permanently at Grasmere and as the influence of his sister became even stronger on him, the way in which he responded to and interpreted Nature in his poetry underwent a profound change. Nowhere is this more clear than in the changes to be seen between *Lyrical Ballads*, especially the second edition of 1801 with the inclusion of *Tintern Abbey*, and the publication, *Poems in Two Volumes*, in May 1807. Between the two, Wordsworth had continued work on *The Prelude* and had completed the first version by May 1805 as well as having written most of the other 'philosophical' poems that we associate with him, e.g. *Resolution and Independence* and *Ode on Intimations of Immortality*. But most of the nature poems that we associate with

Wordsworth, including the 'Daffodils', the really famous and much anthologized poems, are to be found in the two volumes of 1807. As so often, it is Wordsworth himself who best describes the change that had come about in him and the part that his sister played in it:

> *Child of my Parents! Sister of my Soul!*
> *Elsewhere have strains of gratitude been breathed*
> *To thee for all the early tenderness*
> *Which I from thee imbibed: and true it is*
> *That later seasons owed to thee no less: ...*
> *Even to the very going-out of youth,*
> *The period which our story now hath reached,*
> *I too exclusively esteemed that love,*
> *And sought that beauty, which, as Milton sings,*
> *Hath terror in it. Thou didst soften down*
> *This over-sterness; but for thee, sweet Friend!*
> *My soul, too reckless of mild grace, had been*
> *Far longer what by Nature it was framed,*
> *Longer retained its countenance severe,*
> *A rock with torrents roaring, with the clouds*
> *Familiar, and a favourite of the stars:*
> *But thou didst plant its crevices with flowers,*
> *Hang it with shrubs that twinkle in the breeze,*
> *And teach the little birds to build their nests*
> *And warble in its chambers.*[17]

On William and Dorothy's long walks together (they have even been described as the first hikers and they certainly covered remarkable distances) Nature became transformed into an ever-present joy, a source of comfort and of ever-changing, though often minute, delights. The change was from the contemplation of the 'roaring torrents' to that of the daisy, the green-linnet, the skylark, the small celandine, and the other poems of 'the fancy' as Wordsworth called them in arranging their order in his *Collected Edition* of 1815. This classification is important, it marks them as apart from the 'poems of the Imagination' which were generally more ambitious and more concerned with the identification of the harmony of things through the power of the human mind that we have been discussing.

Not all the *Poems in Two Volumes* were of 'the fancy' (the famous 'Daffodils' was itself classified as a poem of 'the imagination') but almost all of them owe much of their origin,

Silhouette of Dorothy
Wordsworth, thought
to be the only known
likeness of her as a
young woman
(Reproduced by
courtesy of the
Trustees of Dove
Cottage)

and many of their images, to Dorothy herself. We may see these
volumes almost as the result of a literary and personal
collaboration between them. Nowhere does this emerge more
clearly than in Dorothy Wordsworth's *Journals*,[18] especially those
written at Grasmere. Delightful reading in themselves they are
essential material for anyone wanting to understand the
Wordsworths at this time. It was a hard but satisfying life they
appeared to have led, a time, as Wordsworth was to call it, of
'plain living and high thinking'. They shared the 'plain living' —
their main diet appears to have been porridge which they had for
both supper and breakfast and peas which they grew themselves.
It is still legendary in Grasmere that they suffered throughout
their lives from chronic indigestion but much of the hard work
appears to have been done by Dorothy. Her *Journals* contain
what, looking back on them, seem many amusing insights into
the nature of their life together. Here are a couple of days in
August 1800 for example:

Friday 21st. *Very cold. Baking in the morning, gathered
pea seeds and took up — lighted a fire upstairs. Walked as*

> *far as Rydale with John intending to have gone on to Ambleside but we found the papers at Rydale—Wm walking in the wood all the time. John and he went out after our return—I mended stockings. Wind very high shaking the corn.*
>
> Saturday 22nd. *A very fine morning. Wm was composing all the morning. I shelled peas, gathered beans, and worked in the garden till ½ past 12 then walked with William in the wood. The Gleams of sunshine and the stirring trees and gleaming boughs, cheerful lake, most delightful. After dinner we walked to Ambleside—showery—went to see Mr Partridge's house. Came home by Clappersgate. We had intended going by Rydale woods, but it was cold—I was not well, and tired. Got tea immediately and had a fire. Did not reach home until 7 o'clock—mended stockings—and W. read Peter Bell. He read us the poem of Joanna beside the Rothay by the roadside.*

The adoring sister was often, understandably, ill and tired but she records in great detail the progress of her brother's compositions of his poems and her own detailed observation of the Nature around her. Many of these observations later became worked into the poems. Perhaps most striking, because of our familiarity with the poem, is *her* account of the sight of the daffodils at Ullswater. In April 1802 she wrote:

> Thursday 15th. *When we were in the woods beyond Gowbarrow park we saw a few daffodils close to the water side. We fancied that the lake had floated the seeds ashore and that the little colony had so sprung up. But as we went along there were more and yet more and at last under the boughs of the trees, we saw that there was a long belt of them (the end we did not see)* along the shore, about the breadth of a country turnpike road. I never saw daffodils so beautiful they grew among the mossy stones about and about them some rested their heads upon these stones as on a pillow for weariness and the rest tossed and reeled and danced and seemed as if they verily laughed with the wind that blew upon them, they looked so gay ever glancing ever changing.*

---

* These six words are erased in the final version but have a clear relevance to Wordsworth's '*They stretched in never-ending line*'.

Dorothy's *Journals* are remarkable for the keenness of their observations, the persistent patience she had in dealing with her often difficult brother, and the housewifely good sense that comes through in every page. They prove beyond all doubt the importance of her influence over Wordsworth in this period of his creative life and the fact that it was she who taught him to look at Nature with a new eye and 'soften down' his 'oversterness'. To her influence most of the *Poems in Two Volumes* may be attributed.

It was suggested earlier that the 'Daffodils' is by no means as simple a poem as it might seem at first sight, especially because of its overfamiliarity. Try reading it again alongside the account by Dorothy which has just been given. Note where Wordsworth has changed things in the final version. Even the first line marks a conscious change: '*I wandered lonely as a cloud*' —yet we know, in fact, that it was an experience shared by the two of them. But the evocation of loneliness, the creation of the mood which will be re-created at the end of the poem '*in vacant or in pensive mood*' is part of the process of embellishment, of Art improving upon Nature that was characteristic of the picturesque as practiced throughout by Wordsworth. As in the earlier poems (and fitting this one, too, to be classified as a poem of 'the imagination') it is not until later that the real significance of the experience is understood. As in *Tintern Abbey* it is the recollection, the use the mind can make of the experience in its contemplation of the universe, that is the central experience of the poem:

> *I gazed—and gazed—but little thought*
> *What wealth the show to me had brought:*
>
> *For oft, when on my couch I lie*
> *In vacant or in pensive mood,*
> *They flash upon that inward eye*
> *Which is the bliss of solitude ;*
> *And then my heart with pleasure fills*
> *And dances with the daffodils.*[19]

The apt and powerful description is that of Dorothy—it is remarkable how closely the first two stanzas of the poem relate to her notebook entry—but the use made of the experience, its transformation, is the work of the poet and the poetic imagination. Only when he is read thus, can the real significance of Wordsworth as a poet of Nature be appreciated.[20]

Wordsworth himself valued the poem very highly and spoke of it as having that '*property and right which love and knowledge confer*'. The use of the word 'knowledge' is important; it is the same knowledge that is seen and felt and understood in *Tintern Abbey*, the knowledge of the imagination. In many ways the most remarkable thing about Wordsworth at his best is his ability to combine extraordinary and accurate close observation of detail with this sense of something going beyond the everyday. One could use his poetry, even today, as a guidebook to the places it describes. While working on this book I walked with friends along the course of the River Duddon with the sonnet sequence in my hands. As we came to Ulpha Church we were puzzled that we could not at first see how the poet could have written there of 'that wave-washed Churchyard' until we realized that we were approaching it from the wrong direction. If we had walked, as Wordsworth had done, from the source to the mouth instead of in the reverse direction we would have found his description immediately accurate. But the accuracy is always informed by the picturesque style and this perfect sonnet is a very good example of the scene painting in which this poetry so frequently engages.

On the same excursion it was a matter of considerable excitement to stand in Grasmere and to follow the directions carefully to find the exact spot where Michael's cottage had stood. The directions are more adequate than many a modern guidebook:

> *If from the public way you turn your steps*
> *Up the tumultuous brook of Green-head Ghyll,*
> *You will suppose that with an upright path*
> *Your feet must struggle ; in such bold ascent*
> *The pastoral mountains front you, face to face.*
> *But, courage! for around that boisterous brook*
> *The mountains have all opened out themselves,*
> *And made a hidden valley of their own.*
> *No habitation can be seen ; but they*
> *Who journey thither find themselves alone*
> *With a few sheep, with rocks and stones, and kites*
> *That overhead are sailing in the sky.*[21]

The story that Wordsworth tells of the old shepherd, Michael, and his prodigal son is doubtless one that had lived on in the memory of the people of Grasmere from whom Wordsworth heard it, as indeed he tells us:

I have conversed with more than one who well
Remember the old Man [22]

and of the actual physical reality of Michael there is no doubt.
He comes vividly to life, with his wife and son, Luke, in the
poem. There is about him the same truth to detail as we
discovered in the physical descriptions of landscape. But as the
poem moves towards its majestic ending Michael becomes more
than this alone; like so many of Wordsworth's rustic figures he
becomes transformed (again by the power of the imagination) to
something beyond himself. While never losing his reality as an
actual person he also becomes a symbol including within him all
the suffering of old age, of infirmity, of parents deserted by their
children, of fond hopes dashed, of pride as well as suffering, and
of the plight of the countryman in a time of change and
enclosure:

> *There, by the Sheep-fold, sometimes was he seen*
> *Sitting alone, or with his faithful Dog,*
> *Then old, beside him, lying at his feet.*
> *The length of full seven years, from time to time,*
> *He at the building of this Sheep-fold wrought,*
> *And left the work unfinished when he died.*
> *Three years, or little more, did Isabel*
> *Survive her Husband: at her death the estate*
> *Was sold, and went into a stranger's hand.*
> *The cottage which was named the EVENING STAR*
> *Is gone—the ploughshare has been through the ground*
> *On which it stood; great changes have been wrought*
> *In all the neighbourhood:—yet the oak is left*
> *That grew beside their door; and the remains*
> *Of the unfinished Sheep-fold may be seen*
> *Beside the boisterous brook of Green-head Ghyll.* [23]

All of Wordsworth's extraordinary qualities as a poet come
together here. There is the conscious narrative art, the ability to
bring us back with a word ('boisterous') at the end to where we
began the story nearly 500 lines previously; the sense of
continuity in the landscape alongside the coming of inevitable
change; above all, the twin notes of melancholy and acceptance at
the end. Rarely have the 'simple annals of the poor' had so
faithful a chronicler.

5

Frequently in this account of Wordsworth and Nature reference has been made to the art of gardening. This is in itself of considerable importance. Wordsworth was a keen and expert gardener and the art of taming Nature in a garden whilst retaining its natural qualities is itself a part of the picturesque movement. The art of gardening is directly analogous to that of poetry in Wordworth's view and he is reputed to have said that he thought himself endowed by Nature with the qualities needed for success in the three related callings of poet, landscape gardener and critic of works of art. He created three great gardens in all: that at Dove Cottage (the Orchard Garden), the Winter Garden at Coleorton Hall which he designed for Lord and Lady Beaumont (now largely destroyed in its original conception), and the garden at Rydal Mount. The first and the last of these remain largely as their creator had intended and they stand out still today as a tribute to his skill in the art. Of the garden at Dove Cottage he remarks with understandable pride '*A Poet made it*' and as he is leaving for two months away he takes a farewell that brings home something of what it meant to him:

Farewell, thou little Nook of mountain-ground
Thou rocky corner in the lowest stair

The Wordsworths' garden at Dove Cottage (Esmor Jones)

Of that magnificent temple which doth bound
One side of our whole vale with grandeur rare;
Sweet garden-orchard, eminently fair,
The loveliest spot that man hath ever found,
Farewell! —we leave thee to Heaven's peaceful care,
Thee, and the Cottage which thou dost surround.[24]

Wordsworth's own principles of gardening are set out most
clearly in a letter to Sir George Beaumont of 17th October 1805
and in Part III of his 1810 *Guide to the English Lakes*. In the
letter he makes the highest claims for the art of gardening:

All just and solid pleasure in natural objects rest upon two
pillars, God and Man. Laying out grounds, as it is called,
may be considered as a liberal art, in some sort like Poetry
and Painting; and its object, like that of all the liberal arts,
is, or ought to be, to move the affections under the control of
good sense; that is, of the best and wisest, but speaking with
more precision, it is to assist Nature in moving the affections
…No liberal art aims merely at the gratification of an
individual or a class, the Painter or Poet is degraded in
proportion as he does so; the true servants of the Arts pay
homage to human kind as impersonated in unwarped and
enlightened minds. If this be so when we are merely putting
together words or colours, how much more ought the feeling
to prevail when we are in the midst of the realities of
things; of the beauty and harmony, of the joy and
happiness, of living creatures; of men and children, of birds
and beasts, of hills and streams, and trees and flowers; with
the changes of night and day, evening and morning, summer
and winter; and with all their unwearied actions and
energies, as benign in the spirit which animates them as they
are beautiful and grand in that form and clothing which is
given them for the delight of our senses.

In his *Guide to the English Lakes* Wordsworth fights an
increasing battle against newcomers who would destroy the
beauty of the area by adding buildings that do not blend
harmoniously with the landscape or who chop down native
woodlands. One of his strongest objections to the coming of the
Kendal and Windermere Railway was that its construction would
mean the felling of a number of trees that in his view ought to be
protected. There is also a splendid account of the poet planting

holly trees (of which he was exceedingly fond) for posterity in his seventy-third year:

> *Wordsworth was in a very happy, kindly mood. We took a walk on the terrace, and he went as usual to his favourite points. On our return he was struck by the berries on the holly tree, and said, 'Why should not you and I go and pull some berries ... and then we can go and plant them in the rocky ground behind the house.' We pulled the berries, and set forth with our tool. I made the holes, and the poet put in the berries. He was as earnest and eager about it as if it had been a matter of importance; and as he put the seeds in, he every now and then muttered, in his low solemn tone, that beautiful verse from Burns'* Vision—

And wear thou this, she solemn said,
And bound the holly round my head.
The polished leaves and berries red
   Did rustling play;
And like a passing thought she fled
   In light away.

> *He clambered to the highest rocks ... and put in the berries in such situations as Nature sometimes does with such true and beautiful effect. He said 'I like to do this for posterity'.*[25]

His basic principle for gardening was in many ways identical with his prescription for poetry: '*The rule is simple: with respect to grounds—work, where you can, in the spirit of Nature, with an invisible hand of art.*' In all of this, in fact, '*let the images of Nature be your guide.*'

Just as Wordsworth was an enthusiastic gardener who constructed his gardens with a full knowledge of the latest discussion of the principles of landscaping so, too, he was an informed art critic and a collector of taste himself. His own interests in art had been formed by Sir George Beaumont and the contemporary fashions that we have been describing and he came to have clear principles on which to base his judgments. Here he is, for example, writing to Sir George Beaumont in 1811 on the subject of Rubens' painting of *Castle Steen* and arguing for something very much based upon the principle of the picturesque:

The artist and his friends at *Castle Steen* by Sir Peter Paul Rubens
(Kunsthistorisches Museum, Vienna)

> *I heard the other day of two artists who thus expressed*
> *themselves upon the subject of a scene among our Lakes.*
> *'Plague upon those vile Enclosures!' said One; 'they spoil*
> *everything.' 'O,' said the Other, 'I never see them.' ... Now,*
> *for my part, I should not wish to be either of the Gentlemen,*
> *but to have in my own mind the power of turning to*
> *advantage, whereever it is possible, every object of Art and*
> *Nature as they appear before me. What a noble instance, as*
> *you have often pointed out to me, has Rubens given of this*
> *in that picture in your possession, where he has brought, as*
> *it were, a whole County into one Landscape, and made the*
> *most formal partitions of cultivation; hedge-rows of pollard*
> *willows conduct the eye with the depths and distances of his*
> *picture; and thus, more than by any other means, has given*
> *it that appearance of immensity which is so striking.*

Certain fundamental laws apply to the arts of gardening,
painting and poetry alike and the most essential of these is that
'*the invisible hand of art should everywhere work in the spirit of*
Nature; Nature is itself essentially the Art of God and the poet
must be first true to that in following his own inspiration'. The poet
is urged to let:

> *Thy Art be Nature; ...*
> *How does the Meadow-flower its bloom unfold?*
> *Because the lovely little flower is free*
> *Down to its root, and, in that freedom, bold;*
> *And so the grandeur of the Forest-tree*
> *Comes not by casting in a formal mould,*
> *But from its own divine vitality.*[26]

He frequently draws a parallel between painting and poetry and
insists that in both cases success comes primarily through hard
work and effort in the attempt to capture the truth that
Nature provides as a model:

> *Creative Art*
> *(Whether the instrument of words she use,*
> *Or pencil pregnant with ethereal hues,)*
> *Demands the service of a mind and heart,*
> *Though sensitive, yet, in their weakest part,*
> *Heroically fashioned ...*
> *Great is the glory, for the strife is hard!*[27]

The analogy already made with the modern art of photography is made clear in a sonnet, *Upon the sight of a beautiful picture*, that Wordsworth wrote on Sir George Beaumont's picture of Coleorton landscape where he stresses the significance of the painting (or for that matter the poem) being able to 'fix' a moment in time. True to his general principles he modifies the details in the painting that he has in front of him to make a poem that is essentially his own and he tells us that the images of the smoke and the travellers are the only ones actually taken from Beaumont's painting. The rest were added *'for the sake of variety'*:

> *Praised be the Art whose subtle power could stay*
> *Yon cloud, and fix it in that glorious shape;*
> *Nor would permit the thin smoke to escape,*
> *Nor those bright sunbeams to forsake the day;*
> *Which stopped that band of travellers on their way,*
> *Ere they were lost within the shady wood;*
> *And showed the Bark upon the glassy flood*
> *For ever anchored in her sheltering bay.*
> *Soul-soothing Art! whom Morning, Noontide, Even,*
> *Do serve with all their changeful pageantry;*
> *Thou, with ambition modest yet sublime,*
> *Here, for the sight of mortal man, hast given*
> *To one brief moment caught from fleeting time*
> *The appropriate calm of blest eternity.*

Although the early Wordsworth is inspired by such sights as the Simplon Pass to thoughts of the sublime it is, in the end, the picturesque that is the aspect of Nature that he is most fascinated by. There is a comforting, almost womb-like air to the countryside around Grasmere for example; the natural beauty there is never threatening and it is to this countryside that he returns again and again in his writing. Even in the tours to the continent and Scotland it is countryside most like that of Grasmere that catches his eye; as one travels today down the course of the Yarrow one recognizes just how at home Wordsworth must have felt in visiting such spots. In the fine sequence of poems that he writes celebrating a walk along the course of the River Duddon it is the miniature, the picturesque, elements in the scene that he keeps on referring to with pleasure and delight:

Buttermere and the Fells in the Lake District (Esmor Jones)

> *Not hurled precipitous from steep to steep;*
> *Lingering no more 'mid flower-enamelled lands*
> *And blooming tickets; nor by rocky bands*
> *Held; but in a radiant progress toward the Deep*
> *Where mightiest rivers, into powerless sleep*
> *Sink, and forget their nature—now expands*
> *Majestic Duddon, over smooth flat sands*
> *Gliding in silence with unfettered sleep!*
> *Beneath an ampler sky a region wide*
> *Is opened round him:—hamlets, towers, and towns,*
> *And blue-topped hills, behold him from afar;*
> *In stately mien to sovereign Thames allied*
> *Spreading his bosom under Kentish downs,*
> *With commerce freighted, or triumphant war.*[28]

Two of Wordsworth's favourite devices in gardening relate directly to his work as a poet. In all his gardens, but especially at Coleorton, he wrote poems to be inscribed on native stone to decorate the gardens and to commemorate his friends. In Coleorton, for example, in some lines written in honour of Sir George Beaumont, he writes in *The Embowering Rose:*

> *Here may some Painter sit in future days,*
> *Some future Poet meditate his lays;*
> *Not mindless of that distant age renowned*
> *When Inspiration hovered o'er this ground.*

Near Rydal Mount there is a stone on which is written verses in which Wordsworth commemorates his intervention to protect the countryside:

> *In these fair Vales, hath many a tree*
> *At Wordsworth's suit been spared,*
> *And from the builder's hand this Stone,*
> *For some rude beauty of its own,*
> *Was rescued by the Bard ;*
> *Long may it rest in peace! and here*
> *Perchance the tender-hearted*
> *Will heave a gentle sigh for him*
> *As One of the Departed.*

It is perhaps appropriate that one of the yew trees near his grave in Grasmere churchyard was planted by his own hand.

The other feature of Wordsworth's gardens that links with his writing was the characteristic building of terraces up and down which he could pace in the composition of his works. Both Dove Cottage and Rydal Mount still show evidence of his efforts here and the feeling he had for them is summed up in words he wrote when in 1826 he thought that he was to leave Rydal Mount and is taking farewell of his terrace:

> *Yet on the mountain's side*
> *A Poet's hand first shaped it ; and the steps*
> *Of that same Bard—repeated to and fro*
> *At morn, at noon, and under moonlight skies*
> *Through the vicissitudes of many a year—*
> *Forbade the weeds to creep o'er its grey line.*
> *No longer, scattering to the heedless winds*
> *The vocal raptures of fresh poesy,*
> *Shall he frequent these precincts ; locked no more*
> *In earnest converse with beloved Friends,*
> *Here will he gather stores of ready bliss,*
> *As from the beds and borders of a garden*
> *Choice flowers are gathered!*[29]

At Dove Cottage the Poet was accustomed to refer to the garden as 'his study'; anyone who visits it today will still recapture some of this feeling and have a real insight into what Nature meant so far as Wordsworth was concerned.

[1]From *The Moralists* written 1709, published 1711.   [2]Russell Noyes *Wordsworth and the Art of Landscape* (Indiana U.P., Bloomington, 1968) p. 6   [3]Thomas Gray *The Bard* ll 15–22   [4]William Wordsworth *The Prelude* (1850 version) Bk VI ll 624–40   [5]William Wordsworth *An Evening Walk* ll 98–113   [6]As 2 p. 11   [7]James Thomson *The Seasons* (Autumn) ll 1080–1100   [8]As 4 (1805 version) Bk VIII ll 81–110   [9]*ibid.* Bk IV ll 329–345   [10]William Wordsworth *Lines composed a few miles above Tintern Abbey* ll 4–14   [11]*ibid.* ll 50–7   [12]*ibid.* ll 102–11   [13]*ibid.* ll 36–49   [14]As 4 (1805 version) Bk III ll 124–8   [15]*ibid.* Bk I ll 351–71   [16]Basil Willey *The Eighteenth Century Background* (Chatto and Windus, 1940) p. 276   [17]As 4 (1805 version) Bk XIII ll 211–36   [18]Dorothy Wordsworth *Journals* ed. Mary Moorman (O.U.P., 1971)   [19]William Wordsworth *I Wandered Lonely as a Cloud* ll 17–24   [20]For a more detailed and thought-provoking analysis of this poem, see Geoffrey Durrant *William Wordsworth* (Cambridge U.P., 1969) pp. 18–33   [21]William Wordsworth *Michael* ll 1–12   [22]*ibid.* ll 451–2   [23]*ibid.* ll 467–82   [24]William Wordsworth *A Farewell* ll 1–8   [25]As 2 p. 138   [26]William Wordsworth *A Poet* ll 5–14   [27]William Wordsworth *Sonnet to Haydon* ll 1–14   [28]William Wordsworth 'Not hurled precipitous from steep to steep' ll 1–14 (sonnet number XXXII in *The River Duddon* sequence)   [29]William Wordsworth *The Massy Ways Carried Across These Heights* ll 5–17

4

Wordsworth as Critic

As much in the area of literary criticism as that of poetry, Wordsworth forms a bridge between the eighteenth century and our own times. The Advertisement to *Lyrical Ballads* in 1798 is consciously written to defend a new style of poetry which seeks to repair some of the excesses of the poetry fashionable at the time:

> *The majority of the following poems are to be considered as experiments. They were written chiefly with a view to ascertain how far the language of conversation in the middle and lower classes of society is adapted to the purposes of poetic pleasure. Readers accustomed to the gaudiness and inane phraseology of many modern writers ... will perhaps frequently have to struggle with feelings of strangeness and awkwardness: they will look round for poetry, and will be induced to enquire by what species of courtesy these attempts can be permitted to assume that title.*

From the very first, then, Wordsworth's criticism is occasional, it seeks to justify and explain his own poetic practice. Although his critical ideas have had an immense influence, there was no carefully worked out 'system'. His ideas sprang more from his own engagement in the task of writing than from any carefully articulated theory of poetry such as a professional critic of today might produce. Nonetheless, there is some consistency to be discovered in his critical writings and this chapter attempts to draw out some of the leading ideas to assist a reading of the poetry rather than concentrating on the critical theories for their own sake.

I

The Advertisement itself was greatly expanded in the two versions of the Preface to Lyrical Ballads that appeared in 1800 and 1802. An examination of these, and of the importance of the differences between them, must be the focal point for any consideration of Wordsworth as a critic, but one other aspect of the Advertisement should be considered first. This emphasizes the importance Wordsworth attributes, perhaps because of his awareness of the seemingly revolutionary character of his poetry, to being able to point to a literary *tradition* to which he belongs.

In the Advertisement Wordsworth makes brief comments on a number of his poems to demonstrate their authenticity. He is clearly already at pains to dispute the charge that his poems are based upon tales and characterizations that have no bearing upon reality:

> *The tale of Goody Blake and Harry Gill is founded on a well-authenticated fact which happened in Warwickshire. Of the other poems in the collection, it may be proper to say that they are either absolute inventions of the author, or facts that took place within his personal observation or that of his friends. The poem of the Thorn, as the reader will soon discover, is not supposed to be spoken in the author's own person: the character of the loquacious narrator will sufficiently shew itself in the course of the story. The Rime of the Ancyent Marinere was professedly written in imitation of the style, as well as the spirit of the elder poets; but with a few exceptions, the Author believes that the language adopted in it has been equally intelligible for these three last centuries.*

The link with the tradition of the past, along with the originality of the 'experiments', together with the concern over language and the problems for the contemporary reader that Wordsworth's chosen language may create, are themes to be returned to in the developed forms of the Preface in 1800 and 1802.

The 1800 Preface made clear that a major preoccupation of the *Lyrical Ballads* was to produce a poetry that would have a quality of permanence that would survive the passage of time. Early in the Preface Wordsworth himself makes the point:

> *Several of my Friends are anxious for the success of these Poems from a belief that, if the views with which they were composed were indeed realized, a class of Poetry would be produced, well adapted to interest mankind permanently, and not unimportant in the multiplicity, and in the quality of its moral relations: and on this account they have*

> *advised me to prefix a systematic defence of the theory upon*
> *which the poems were written.*

How the difficulties that are created by the expectations of readers in different ages may be overcome is the real subject-matter of the *Preface*.

A means towards this quality of permanence was to be found through the subject-matter of the poetry. The content of the poetry is to be drawn from '*incidents and situations from common life*' and it was intended '*to relate or describe them, throughout, as far as was possible, in a selection of language really used by men*'. The reality of the source of the poems is strongly stressed and together with this goes the intention: '*to make these incidents and situations interesting by tracing in them truly though not ostentatiously, the primary laws of our nature.*' Two points emerge here. Firstly, the poetry has a psychological basis: it enables us to understand ourselves better than we would otherwise do; secondly, because the people of the countryside are living more simple lives, it will be easier to observe and understand the '*primary laws of our nature*' by observing them:

> *Low and rustic life was generally chosen, because in that*
> *condition, the essential passions of the heart find a better soil*
> *in which they can attain their maturity, are less under*
> *restraint, and speak a plainer and more emphatic language;*
> *because in that condition of life our elementary feelings co-*
> *exist in a state of greater simplicity, and, consequently, may*
> *be more accurately contemplated, and more forcibly*
> *communicated.*

The occupations of such men of 'rural life' are 'more durable' and their language '*is a more permanent, and a far more philosophical language, than that which is frequently substituted for it by Poets, who ... furnish food for fickle tastes, and fickle appetites, of their own creation.*' The emphasis throughout is upon permanence with at least some suggestion that, because of the largely unchanging nature of their work and their environment, the simple folk of the countryside are the best source for the fundamental and simple truths underlying the variety of human experience.

Although the restatement of these ideas with particular reference to the poems that accompany them is new, the ideas themselves are as much eighteenth century in their origin as

Romantic. The notion that the real purpose of literature is to celebrate the general and permanent aspects of humanity is a commonplace of eighteenth century literary criticism. The most famous statement of it is probably to be found in Dr Johnson: '*Nothing can please many, and please long, but just representations of general nature.*' Or, as he puts it in his moral tale, *Rasselas*:

> The business of the poet is to examine, not the individual, but the species; to remark general properties and large appearances; he does not number the streaks of the tulip, or describe the different shades in the verdure of the forest. He is to exhibit in his portraits of nature such prominent and striking features as recall the original to every mind, and must neglect the minuter discriminations.

There is a good deal of similarity between the expression of these ideas and those of Wordsworth in the Preface of 1800. Indeed, one can hardly escape the view that, at this stage, the countryside and the representatives of 'low and rustic life' are almost seen as the 'laboratory' within which the 'experiments' of the poetry can be conducted. Certainly Wordsworth's attitude has about it something of the patronage of the well-educated gentleman contemplating the primitive life of the countryside. The language of the people is, for example, to be '*purified ... from what appear to be its real defects, from all lasting and rational causes of dislike or disgust*' before it can be adopted to contemplate '*the beautiful and permanent forms of nature*'. The tone throughout the Preface, and even more in the Advertisement, is of a civilized Poet addressing his equally civilized Readers, especially those '*Readers of superior judgement*' and those who are '*more conversant ... with our elder writers.*' The eighteenth century concept of a restricted audience sharing certain assumptions in common with the writer is not left behind at all; rather the intention is to change some of the assumptions, to enable the audience to find an interest in things that they had perhaps taken for granted before. In *The Ancient Mariner* Coleridge sought to make '*strange things familiar*'; in these poems, the intention is that '*ordinary things should be presented to the mind in an unusual way.*'

The other eighteenth century element of the parts of the Preface so far discussed is the concern for the business of the poet being that of *imitation*, an idea that goes all the way back to classical times and the writings of Aristotle. This explains the constant emphasis on truth and reality in the poems. The writer who bases his subject-matter upon the behaviour of a social class to which he does not belong and who adopts a selection from the language of that class as the medium of his poetry, is taking up the stance of an observer, a *'reporter, or imitator of the habits, personal, social, and linguistic, of a body of society to which he does not belong.'*[1] But already with the Preface of 1800 there are one or two suggestions that imply a different theory of poetry which is to be developed considerably in the 1802 version of the Preface. Especially these include the references to poetry as *'the spontaneous overflow of powerful feelings'* and a few other phrases that imply a totally different conception of poetry, one that sees it as concerned, above all, with *expression*, particularly an expression of the mind of the poet himself. This is much more the position of the developed Romantic theory of the later part of the nineteenth century. The 1800 Preface, therefore, seems in this respect to mark a transition between two quite different theories of the nature of poetry. The difficulty that is involved in the statement derives from the use of the word 'spontaneous'. Immediately afterwards, Wordsworth's own gloss upon this, his account of the actual business of poetic composition, provides a less inspirational notion of the poet's task:

> Poetry...takes its origin from emotion recollected in tranquillity: the emotion is contemplated till by a species of reaction the tranquillity gradually disappears, and an emotion, similar to [the 1802 version reads 'kindred to'] that which was before the subject of contemplation, is gradually produced, and does actually exist in the mind.

The task of the Poet is thus not one of pure and slavish imitation alone, his own mind and sensibility are active in the process of creation, the final poem is the outcome not just of observation and response but also of 'contemplation' on the poet's behalf. In his letter to John Wilson of 1802 defending *The Idiot Boy* Wordsworth makes clearer the position towards which he is now moving:

> A great Poet ... ought, to a certain degree, to rectify men's feelings ... to render their feelings more sane, pure and permanent, in short, more consonant to nature ... He ought to travel before men occasionally as well as at their sides ... It is not enough for me as a Poet, to deliniate merely such

feelings as all men do sympathise with; but it is also highly desirable to add to these others, such as all men may sympathise with, and such as there is reason to believe they would be better and more moral beings if they did sympathise with.

Clearly a view is emerging here of the role of the Poet as teacher, one who sees clearer than other men the moral order of the universe and whose moral awarenesses are incorporated in his poetry so as to become a source of enlightenment to others.

A long passage inserted into the 1802 version of the Preface admirably summarizes the position that Wordsworth now seems to have reached:

Taking up the subject, then, upon general grounds, I ask what is meant by the word Poet? What is a Poet? To whom does he address himself? And what language is to be expected from him? He is a man speaking to men: a man, it is true, endued with a more lively sensibility, more enthusiasm and tenderness, who has a greater knowledge of human nature, and a more comprehensive soul, than are supposed to be common among mankind; a man pleased with his own passions and volitions, and who rejoices more than other men in the spirit of life that is in him; delighting to contemplate similar volitions and passions as manifested in the goings-on of the Universe, and habitually impelled to create them where he does not find them. To these qualities he has added a disposition to be affected more than other men by absent things as if they were present; an ability of conjuring up in himself passions, which are indeed far from being the same as those produced by real events, yet ... do more nearly resemble the passions produced by real events, than anything which, other men are accustomed to feel in themselves; whence, and from practice, he has acquired a greater readiness and power in expressing what he thinks and feels, and especially those thoughts and feelings which, by his own choice, or from the stucture of his own mind, arise in him without immediate external excitement.

The whole of the lengthy interpolation in the 1802 Preface from which these sentences are quoted tends to concentrate its interest upon the nature of the task of poetic composition itself, to examine the role played by the Poet as the interpreter and presenter of his subject matter. We have moved away from what was in 1800 predominantly a theory of poetry based upon imitation, a neo-classical conception, to one based upon the idea of expression, something much more recognizably Romantic in its doctrine. M. H. Abrams, in his important book on Romantic critical theory, *The Mirror and the Lamp*, puts it thus:

> *Poetry is the overflow, utterance, or projection of the thought and feelings of the poet* ... *A work of art is essentially the internal made external, resulting from a creative process operating under the impulse of feeling, and embodying the combined product of the poet's perceptions, thoughts, and feelings. The primary source and subject matter of a poem, therefore, are the attributes and actions of the poet's own mind; or if aspects of the external world, then these are only as they are converted from fact to poetry by the feelings and operations of the poet's mind.*[2]

It follows that whatever interests the mind of the Poet can also be the subject-matter for a poem. Wordsworth is himself on record as saying that he could find a poem in anything. In his own day, and since, one of the charges brought against his poetry was often its seeming triviality but for Wordsworth nothing that had engaged his mind, *as Poet*, could conceivably be without interest or merely trivial, whatever its subject-matter.

2

The second major concern of the Prefaces is with the language in which the subject-matter of poetry is to be expressed and, here again, there is a shift in position between the 1800 and 1802 versions. In 1800 the emphasis on the search for permanence again made the language of 'low and rustic life' ('purified of its defects') the most appropriate for poetry. In a deliberate concentration on 'the real language of men' there has had to be a deliberate avoidance of what for the past century had been considered the appropriate language for poetry:

> *There will also be found in these volumes little of what is usually called poetic diction; I have taken as much pains to avoid it as others ordinarily take to produce it; this I have done for the reason already alleged, to bring my language near to the language of men.*

The association of 'the language of men' with the language of the peasant is a further example of the idealization and primitivism that underlies so much of the 1800 Preface but there are other reasons for supposing that this language possesses a unique and permanent quality. The occupations of such people, to begin with, are (or at least seemed to be in Wordsworth's time) 'more durable' and *'the necessary character of rural occupations are more easily comprehended'*.

> *The language of these men is adopted ... because such men hourly communicate with the best objects from which the best part of language is originally derived; and because, from their rank in society and the sameness and narrow circle of their intercourse, being less under the action of social vanity they convey their feelings and notions in simple and unelaborated expressions.*

It is primarily the notion of 'repeated experience and regular feelings' that is attractive here. This may give to the language chosen for *Lyrical Ballads* that feature of permanence that may make them share more in common with the language of Chaucer than their immediate predecessors. However, it is nowhere made very clear exactly what this language is to consist of nor exactly from where it draws its strength. How and why the language of 'rustic folk' should be in any sense a purer language than that of other men remains an unresolved question in the Preface.

There is, however, another attempt to define the language to be used in poetry and this also rejects the accepted poetic diction of the time. After an explicit rejection of the use of *'a large portion of phrases and figures of speech which ... have long been regarded as the common inheritance of Poets,'* Wordsworth goes on to assert that it is the language of prose that is essentially the medium in which to create poetry also.

> *Is there then, it will be asked, no essential difference between the language of prose and metrical composition? I answer that there neither is nor can be any essential difference ... They both speak by and to the same organs.*

However, once again if we are seeking anything positive in the way of definition of this language we are disappointed. At no time in the Preface does Wordsworth seek to make clear, except by negative examples, what are the qualities of this language of prose that he is seeking, and which comes to replace the formula of the language of simple and rustic life in his writing. The conventional poetic diction has been rejected, possibly rightly because it reflects too much the passing fashion of the time, but there is no guarantee that there will be found in the language of prose any greater durability or permanence, nor indeed, in any concrete terms, what that language is going to consist of.

In 1802 the reference to 'the language of prose' is reaffirmed with an even stronger emphasis. But, as in the case of the subject-matter, a new aspect enters into the issue here, that is the effect of the poet himself and the controlling effect he has upon what is written:

> *I answer that the language of such poetry as I am recommending is, as far as is possible, a <u>selection</u> of the language really spoken by men; that this selection, <u>wherever it is made with true taste and feeling</u>, will of itself form a distinction far greater than would at first be imagined, <u>and will entirely separate the composition from the vulgarity and meanness of ordinary life</u>.*
>
> (author's emphasis)

The only real distinction to be made between 'prose' and 'poetry' is on account of metre, a point to which we return later. No other distinction between the language of prose and poetry can be tolerated, especially if the writer is creating dramatic poetry and *'speaks through the mouths of his characters'*:

> *If the Poet's subject be judiciously chosen, it will naturally, and upon fit occasion, lead him to passions the language of which, if selected truly and judiciously, must necessarily be dignified and variegated, and alive with metaphors and figures.*

It is true that, however sensitive the Poet may be, *'the language which it will suggest to him, must, in liveliness and truth, fall far short of that which is uttered by men in real life.'* But even in dramatic poetry the Poet must rely upon *'the principle on which I have so much insisted, namely that of selection; on this he will depend for removing what would otherwise be painful or disgusting in the passion; he will feel that there is no necessity to trick out or to elevate nature.'*

The principle of 'selection' is made even more clear when we consider the case of the Poet speaking in his own person rather than as the presenter of a dramatic characterization. Here we are somewhat close to the conception of the subject-matter of poetry developed in the 1802 Preface. Just as the superiority of the mind and moral understanding of the Poet is the only thing that marks him off from his fellow men so, too, the same applies to his language.

> *Among the qualities which I have enumerated as principally conducing to form a Poet, is implied nothing differing in kind from other men, but only in degree ... The Poet thinks and feels in the spirit of the passions of men. How, then, can his language differ in any material degree from that of all other men who feel vividly and see clearly? It might be* proved *that it is impossible. But supposing this were not the case, the Poet might then be allowed to use a peculiar language when expressing his feelings for his own gratification, or for that of men like himself. But Poets do not write for Poets alone, but for men. ... He must express himself as other men express themselves ... While he is only selecting from the real language of men, or ... composing accurately in the spirit of such selection, he is treading upon safe ground, and we know what we are to expect from him.*

There has been a considerable shift here from what, even in 1800, seemed basically an untenable position. Owen puts it thus:

> *The rustic and his language largely disappear as the poet's norms, the poet himself becomes the representative of general humanity, and his own speech becomes the norm of expression. He expresses his feelings because they are the representative feelings of humanity; and, because his speech is the expression of feeling, its authenticity is assured. Should he have occasion to attribute his speech to persons other than himself, his primary procedure is to identify his feelings with those of such persons. The expressive procedure and the resulting authenticity of language are thus maintained in dramatic poetry.*[3]

In language as in other respects the Poet is the sounding board for humanity.

3

The other major issue dealt with in the Preface is the question of metre which, as we have already noted, Wordsworth sees as the main distinguishing element of poetry as opposed to prose. He himself asks the obvious question: '*Why professing these opinions have I written in verse?*' The answer is a deceptively simple one: he is seeking to avail himself of the source of pleasure that is to be found in metrical language. That the end of poetry should be amongst other things to produce pleasure is, of course, a heartening fact but the source of that pleasure is even more interesting. Wordsworth states the case in terms that seem very close to some aspects of eighteenth century utilitarianism:

> *The end of Poetry is to produce excitement in co-existence with an overbalance of pleasure ... But if the words by which this excitement is produced are in themselves powerful or the images and feelings have an undue proportion of pain connected with them, there is some danger that the excitement may be carried beyond its proper bounds. Now the co-presence of something regular* [i.e. metre] *something to which the mind has been accustomed when in an unexcited state or less excited state, cannot but have great efficacy in tempering and restraining the passion by an intertexture of ordinary feeling.*

In other words, metre acts as a kind of regulator of the emotions. It ensures that in listening to, for example, a tragic tale told in poetry, the pleasure we get from the metrical form overbalances the pain that might result from the tale itself; it also ensures that we are not deceived into mistaking the fictional narrative for reality. The latter point is made clear in an addition in the 1802 version of the Preface:

> *Hence ... the tendency of metre to divest language in a certain degree of reality, and thus to throw a sort of half consciousness of unsubstantial existence over the whole composition, there can be little doubt but that the more pathetic situations and sentiments, that is, those that have a greater proportion of pain connected with them, may be endured in metrical composition, especially in rhyme, than in prose.*

The expression of these ideas in terms of a calculus balancing pain and pleasure so as to ensure an overplus of pleasure in the end is very eighteenth century in its feeling. It derives primarily from the psychological theories of Hartley which we know to have had a strong influence on the early Wordsworth. Hartley's psychology was based upon the association of ideas which he derived from Locke. According to this theory, sense impressions produced vibrations in the brain; two impressions received simultaneously would be linked, and any later recalling of the one would recall the other also. Many of the poems of the early Wordsworth illustrate this psychological theory, notably the 'Poem of the Imagination' entitled *There was a Boy*, which was later incorporated into Book V of *The Prelude*. It is also the whole point of the otherwise trivial poem, *Anecdote for Fathers*, that lying can be taught in infancy by too much pressing for an answer on things which are matters of instinct rather than reason. One aspect of Hartley's theory in which it closely resembles Locke's conception of the mind as a blank sheet of paper on which the world of sensation writes its impressions is that the mind is essentially passive in the act of perception, an idea that Wordsworth develops in *Expostulation and Reply*:

> *The eye — it cannot choose but see;*
> *We cannot bid the ear be still;*
> *Our bodies feel, where'er they be,*
> *Against or with our will.*

> *Nor less I deem that there are Powers*
> *Which of themselves our minds impress;*
> *That we can feed this mind of ours*
> *In a wise passiveness.*[4]

Much of the concept of learning from Nature that informs the earlier books of *The Prelude* derives directly from the same ideas, of course. Certainly Wordsworth's own scheme for the classification of his poetry, which Thomas Hutchinson reproduced in his Oxford edition of 1904 with the comment: '*To it, despite much ridicule and hostile criticism, the poet adhered with unwavering faith throughout the rest of his life*', was constructed on principles based on Hartley's psychology and a poem like *Tintern Abbey* could almost be interpeted as a versification of Hartley's chapter on *The Pleasures and Pains of the Imagination*.

4

Wordsworth did, of course, write a good deal of other literary criticism besides the two versions of the Preface to *Lyrical Ballads* and there is a useful summary of the development of his critical thought, as well as a reprinting of all the relevant texts, in W. J. B. Owen's *Wordsworth's Literary Criticism*. He, too, notes the modernity of much of Wordsworth's thinking and suggests that his '*ideas were not so much adopted by a school as passed into common currency.*' Certainly it is surprising how many of the phrases from the Prefaces that have just been discussed have a familiar ring even to those who have ceased to associate them with the name of Wordsworth. An idea like that of poetry being the spontaneous overflow of powerful feelings has become a commonplace, however startling it may have been when first written and still is, perhaps, when we come to consider the implications that it has. But the details of Wordsworth's critical writings after the Preface of 1802 need not delay us here.

That he was well aware of what he was doing, and that he never had any doubt about his eventual triumph is demonstrated in a personal letter to Lady Beaumont of 21st May, 1807. Here Wordsworth gives eloquent expression to his own feelings about his poems and the purpose of his criticism:

> ... *saving that I have expressed my calm confidence that these Poems will live, I have said nothing which has a particular application to the object of it, which was to remove all disquiet from your mind on account of the condemnation they may at present incur from that portion of my contemporaries who are called the Public ... Be assured that the decision of these persons has nothing to do*

Front view of Rydal Mount (Esmor Jones)

with the Question; they are altogether incompetent judges.
These people in the senseless hurry of their idle lives do not
read books, they merely snatch a glance at them that they
may talk about them. And even if this were not so, never
forget what I believe was observed to you by Coleridge, that
every great and original writer, in proportion as he is great
and original, must himself create the taste by which he is to
be relished; he must teach the art by which he is to be seen
... for this multitude of unhappy, and misguided, and
misguiding beings, an entire regeneration must be pro-
duced; and if this be possible, it must be a work of time.

Time has, in the event, proved Wordsworth to be right and
has vindicated the faith in which he wrote his poems. It may still
be the case that his own criticism, the acute insights that he
expresses there into the processes and the psychology of creation,
are still the best guide that we have to the cultivation of a taste
for his poetry.

[1]W. J. B. Owen *Wordsworth's Literary Criticism* (Routledge & Kegan
Paul, 1974) p. 21 [2]M. H. Abrams *The Mirror and the Lamp* (Norton,
1958) pp. 21–2 [3]W. J. B. Owen *Wordsworth as Critic* (O.U.P., 1969)
p. 113 [4]William Wordsworth *Expostulation and Reply* ll 17–24

5

The Lyrical Ballads

The first volume of this title, called *Lyrical Ballads, with a Few Other Poems*, was published in October 1798, and consisted mainly of poems by Wordsworth, although it also included four by Coleridge, notably *The Ancient Mariner* with which the book opens. The final poem was *Lines composed a few miles above Tintern Abbey*, which was also the last poem to be written and sent to the publisher while the book was in the process of publication. The first edition included an Advertisement which outlined some of the principles upon which the poems were composed. A second edition, in two volumes, of 1800, was published in January 1801 and was entitled *Lyrical Ballads with Other Poems*. It contained the first version of the Preface and, although Volume 1 was substantially the same as the first edition, *The Ancient Mariner* was now placed at the end immediately before *Tintern Abbey*. The whole of Volume 2 consists of poems by Wordsworth himself and is the product of his walking tour of Germany with Dorothy Wordsworth and the early months of their settling at Town End, Grasmere (Dove Cottage). The second volume includes many of Wordsworth's best known and most admired poems such as *Michael, Nutting*, and *The Old Cumberland Beggar*, together with the '*Lucy*' cycle of poems.

The authorship is now attributed solely to W. Wordsworth; the first edition had been published anonymously. The second edition was reprinted in 1802, with the revised and enlarged Preface, and again in 1805. The contemporary reception of these two editions is looked at in Chapter 8; here we are concerned with the nature of the volumes as seen by their authors, and also with some of the essential differences between the two editions. There is no doubt that the original conception was a joint one of Wordsworth and Coleridge; the book was intended to meet the expenses of a walking tour together. However, the one solid outcome of that enterprise was *The Ancient Mariner* and most of Wordsworth's contributions were written without the direct collaboration of Coleridge. There is, however, no doubt that their constant companionship at this time and the many discussions they had together were a major influence on this stage of Wordsworth's career. Much more than the second edition, therefore, the 1798 edition can be seen as a *joint* production of the two poets and there is evidence that this is how they looked at it also. Their Bristol publisher, Cottle, with whom Coleridge had opened up the negotiations, certainly thought of it like this and the volume had been sold to him as a joint venture. From the first, Wordsworth appears to have been the more anxious of the two for the success of the poems, both in terms of their critical reception and the money that would result from their sale. Great though the importance may have been that he placed on poetry, and his own poetry in particular, he was always conscious of working in a commercial market and was never unaware of the financial implications of his work. Almost as soon as he returned to England from Germany, about six months after the original publication, we find him writing to Cottle:

> *You tell me the poems have not sold ill. If it is possible, I should wish to know* what number *have been sold. From what I can gather it seems that* The Ancient Mariner *has upon the whole been an injury to the volume, I mean that the old words and the strangeness of it have deterred readers from going on.*

A month later he is writing to Cottle again to ask for more precise information about the actual sales and he is already showing a sensitiveness to reviews. He was particularly hurt by Southey's comments published in *The Critical Review* of October 1798 and his expression of his disappointment is interesting:

> *Southey's review I have seen. He knew that I published those poems for money and money alone. He knew that money was of importance to me. If he could not conscientiously have spoken differently of the volume, he ought to have declined the task of reviewing it.*
>
> *The bulk of the poems he has described as destitute of merit. Am I recompensed for this by vague praises of my talents? I care little for the praise of any other professional critic, but as it may help me to pudding . . .*

Although there is little reason to doubt the genuineness of Wordsworth's concern with 'pudding' here, it is also certain that these words conceal strong artistic disappointment. The poems had been described in the Advertisement as 'experiments', the anonymity of the publication had, perhaps, been a piece of self-defence in case the experiment did not succeed as hoped for, and in Southey's criticisms he found his fears being fulfilled. Southey was a critic whom Wordsworth respected and whom he might have expected to be capable of understanding his intentions. Considering the deliberate invitation that the Advertisement provided to consider the more revolutionary aspects of the volume, Southey's review, in retrospect, does not seem to have been all that hostile. He begins by quoting Wordsworth's own statements from the Advertisement and taking up the argument at this point:

> *With that which is entitled 'The Thorn', we were altogether displeased ... The author should have recollected that he who personates tiresome loquacity, becomes tiresome himself ... The story of a man who suffers the perpetual pain of cold, because an old woman prayed that he might never be warm, is perhaps a good story for a ballad, because it is a well-known tale: but is the author certain that it is 'well authenticated'? And does not such an assertion promote the popular superstition of witchcraft?*

The comments upon *The Ancient Mariner* are particularly severe and doubtless led to Wordsworth's own misgivings expressed above and the decision to relegate the poem to the end of the reprinted volume of 1800:

> *Many of the stanzas are laboriously beautiful; but in connection they are absurd or unintelligible. ... We do not sufficiently understand the story to analyse it ... Genius has here been employed in producing a poem of little merit.*

Yet, in spite of these strictures, the conclusions are not all that unsatisfying—or should not have been so to an author trying to bring about a revolution in poetic taste:

> *The 'experiment', we think, has failed, not because the language of conversation is little adapted to 'the purposes of poetic pleasure', but because it has been tried upon uninteresting subjects. Yet every piece discovers genius; and, ill as the author has frequently employed his talents, they certainly rank him with the best of living poets.*

For a young writer one might have thought this reasonable enough praise from a well-established critic, but Southey's strictures rankled greatly and not only led to the rearrangements of the second edition but also to the expansion of the Advertisement into the Preface. Wordsworth's own conviction of his talents and his determination to stand by what he knew to be the direction that poetry ought to take, was hardened by the kind of comment quoted here. *The Idiot Boy*, in particular, became, for him, a test piece. To a large extent one's response to that poem became an index of one's response to the whole volume and the approach to poetry that it implied.

Coleridge's own more famous account in Chapter XIV of *Biographia Literaria* of the '*occasion of the* Lyrical Ballads, *and the objects originally proposed*' is very different from that given by Wordsworth at any time and, being mainly the product of the years 1815–17, has the benefit of hindsight. One suspects that it is much more concerned with his view of the purposes of poetry than Wordsworth's even at the time that the poems were originally conceived. It is certainly a much more *philosophical* point of view and more concerned with content than with form and diction:

> *The thought suggested itself (to which of us I do not recollect) that a series of poems might be composed of two sorts. In the one, the incidents and agents were to be, in part at least, supernatural; and the excellence aimed at was to consist in the interesting of the affections by the dramatic truth of such emotions, as would naturally accompany such situations, supposing them real ... For the second class, subjects were to be chosen from ordinary life; the characters and incidents were to be such, as will be found in every village and its vicinity, where there is a meditative and feeling mind to seek after them or to notice them, when they present themselves ... It was agreed, that my endeavours should be directed to persons and characters supernatural, or at least romantic ... so as ... to procure for these shadows of imagination that willing suspension of disbelief for a moment, which constitutes poetic faith.*
>
> *Mr Wordsworth, on the other hand, was to propose to himself as his object, to give the charm of novelty to things of every day, and to excite a feeling analogous to the supernatural, by awakening the mind's attention from the*

lethargy of custom, and directing it to the loveliness and the wonders of the world before us; an inexhaustible treasure, but for which, in consequence of the film of familiarity and selfish solicitude we have eyes, yet see not, ears that hear not, and hearts that neither feel nor understand.

It is clear even from the language in which these ideas are expressed that the conception of the poems proposed by Coleridge was very different from that expressed by Wordsworth in the Advertisement, and even more so in the Preface. This is a point that Coleridge, although generously praising his collaborator's industry as compared with his own, does not forbear to make:

The 'Lyrical Ballads' were published . . . and were presented by him, as an experiment *. . . To the second edition he added a preface of considerable length; in which, notwithstanding some passages of apparently a contrary import, he was understood to contend for the extension of this style of poetry of all kinds, and to reject as vicious and indefensible all phrases and forms of style that were not included in what he (unfortunately, I think, adopting an equivocal expression) called the language of* real *life. From this preface, prefixed to poems in which it was impossible to deny the presence of original genius, however mistaken its direction might be deemed, arose the whole long-continued controversy.*

Coleridge goes on to say that '*with many parts of this preface . . . I never concurred*', and in the rest of the chapter proceeds to explain his own poetic creed so that it may be made clear, once and for all, where he agrees and where he disagrees with the position so polemically adopted by Wordsworth. He does, however, point out—and it is an important point to make—that if a large number of readers had not found something sympathetic and interesting in the poems they would have '*sunk at once, a dead weight, into the slough of oblivion, and have dragged the preface along with them*'. Some of Wordsworth's reviewers might object but '*had Mr Wordsworth's poems been the silly, the childish things, which they were for a long time described as being*' they would not have survived, nor, indeed, would *Lyrical Ballads* have gone through so many quickly reprinted editions.

All this establishes quite clearly that however much there may have been an original intention of a full collaboration on *Lyrical Ballads*, the final outcome and the controversy that resulted is one for which Wordsworth must take full responsibility and this was recognized by the two authors themselves.

We ought, therefore, to ask how original the Wordsworthian contributions to *Lyrical Ballads* were and in what sense the term 'experiments' can properly be applied to them. What can be seen as the characteristic poetic method of these poems?

An important secondary source is Robert Mayo's essay, *The Contemporaneity of the 'Lyrical Ballads'* (1954). He examines the Ballads from the standpoint of the general taste for poetry in the 1790's and seeks to show that, if one compares them with other poems being published in the magazines of the time, they were not as revolutionary as all that. He sets out to show that *'they not only conformed in numerous ways to the modes of 1798 and reflected popular tastes and attitudes, but enjoyed a certain popularity in the magazines themselves.'* He refers to Wordsworth's repeated statements that he wrote the Ballads in order 'to make money' and his fears that the inclusion of the oddity of *The Ancient Mariner* with its 'old words' had hurt the sales of the volume. Hence its relegation in the second edition in which he *'would put in its place some little things which would be more likely to suit the common taste.'* Mayo points to the wide market for poetry publication at the turn of the century, a period that he calls one of a 'poetic inflation', and the plagiarism that went on between one magazine and another. The *Lyrical Ballads* themselves were raided in this manner by half a dozen magazines and therefore *'the general acquaintance with* Goody Blake, We are Seven, *and other poems in the volume cannot be guaged by the number of copies of the original publication in circulation'.*

It is true that the general taste of the time, and the most frequently produced poetry, was exactly of the kind that Wordsworth attacks in the Advertisement in his reference to *'the gaudiness and inane phraseology of many modern writers'* but along with imitations of Gray and Pope are to be found a 'persistent minority' of poems more in the style of the later eighteenth century. Two aspects in particular may be noted: a drift towards Nature and simplicity and also towards a sentimental morality. Mayo concludes that *'considered as a species of poetry, the "nature" poems of the* Lyrical Ballads *were anything but surprising in 1798.'* He comments upon the fact that while *The Ancient Mariner* was regarded by reviewers as a very strange and original poem which sharply divided them over its merits, *Tintern Abbey* is universally regarded with praise. It was described, for example, by Dr Burney as being '*The reflections of no common mind; poetical, beautiful, and philosophical.*' In a very comprehensive survey of the reprinting of poems from *Lyrical Ballads* in the period 1798–1800, Mayo comes to some very startling conclusions:

> *Ten of the twenty-three poems ... were reprinted in full in eight different magazines—some poems more than once; and if we extend our list to cover all the observed reprintings in British magazines in the four years between 1798 and 1802, we can cite a total of 23 from the first two editions (including 15 different poems), 20 of which were specifically identified as coming from the* Lyrical Ballads *or (after 1800) 'Wordsworth's Poems' ... We have an audience of very considerable proportions which dwarfs by many thousands the 1,250 to 1,500 purchasers of the first two editions. It seems likely that Wordsworth's reputation in these first years owes far more to the semi-piratical printers of reviews and magazines than to his legitimate publishers.*

Of the poems in the first edition, it is clear that *Goody Blake and Harry Gill* was the most popular and Mayo cites Coleridge's account in the *Biographia* to substantiate the view that there was no intention directly in the poems themselves of carrying out a literary revolution. The Preface, it was true, did give rise to controversy as we have seen; the poems were not so much startlingly original in form or in subject-matter but in the sheer energy with which they were composed. It was their superiority to much other contemporary poetic production rather than their difference from it that distinguished the *Ballads* in their own time and this may still be their outstanding characteristic so far as we are concerned today.

The difficulty for us is to come to the *Ballads* with a freshness of attention that will enable their real force to be recognized. Hazlitt's comment: '*Fools have laughed at, wise men scarcely understand them*' has a truth that still remains. If one takes as a starting point the poem which Wordsworth felt to be the most important and one of the ones that aroused most controversy, *The Idiot Boy*, one can see the method of composition at work. It is easy to laugh at the presentation of the boy himself and at the foolishness of his mother, and the earlier part of the poem to

some extent, with its seemingly artless simplicity, invites us to do
just this. But to do so would be to react with the heartlessness of
the Doctor in the town who rejects Betty Foy's knock at his door
in the night:

> *And now she's at the Doctor's door,*
> *She lifts the knocker, rap, rap, rap;*
> *The Doctor at the casement shows*
> *His glimmering eyes that peep and doze!*
> *And one hand rubs his old night-cap.*
>
> *'Oh Doctor! Doctor! where's my Johnny?'*
> *'I'm here, what is't you want with me?'*
> *'Oh Sir! you know I'm Betty Foy,*
> *And I have lost my poor dear Boy,*
> *You know him—him you often see;*
>
> *He's not so wise as some folks be:'*
> *'The devil take his wisdom!' said*
> *The Doctor, looking somewhat grim,*
> *'What, Woman! should I know of him?'*
> *And, grumbling, he went back to bed!*[1]

Inevitably we are reminded here of the importunate widow
knocking at the door in the New Testament and we can see that
one of the major themes of the poem is human charity: its real
moral core is in the relationship of love and concern that exists
between Betty Foy, her son, Johnny, and her neighbour, Susan
Gale, and the whole poem leads up to the restoration of them all
to each other at the end. They may speak simply, they may act
foolishly, but they are nonetheless united in a mutual concern
that dignifies and gives strength to what they do in contrast to
those, like the Doctor, who are lacking in human sympathy and
understanding. We must not forget Wordsworth's declared
intention of using these poems to extend our moral awareness
and his constant concern at this time with the plight of the
down-and-out as exhibited in *The Prelude* and in his own letters
and writings. His own role in the poem is clearly established as
that of the detached observer, the narrator who distances himself
from the tale that he has to tell.

> *Oh Reader! now that I might tell*
> *What Johnny and his Horse are doing*

What they've been doing all this time,
Oh could I put it into rhyme,
A most delightful tale pursuing![2]

The tone here, and in the stanzas that follow, in a direct address to the reader and a mock confession of the limitation of his powers is very different from that of the ballad stanzas proper in which most of the poem is composed. They have much more of an eighteenth century feel about them; in the bulk of the poem, Wordsworth succeeds in capturing something of the authentic spirit of the genuine ballad and using its apparently artless simplicity to tell his tale. He is using the narrative of the poem as a parable, as an illustration of the moral point that he wants to emerge which is only trite when it is divorced from the poem itself. The moral strength lies in the presentation of the characters, their ordinariness and simplicity, and in our tendency to laugh at them. When we recognize that tendency and see the whole poem in that light our sympathies are extended in the way that Wordsworth clearly intends and which he expressed in his own comments on the poem to John Wilson in his letter of 1802:

> *I can only say that the loathing and disgust which many people have at the sight of an idiot, is a feeling which, though having some foundation in human nature, is not necessarily attached to it in any virtuous degree, but is owing in a great measure to a false delicacy, and, if I may say it without rudeness, a certain want of comprehensiveness of thinking and feeling. Persons in the lower classes of society have little or nothing of this: if an idiot is born in a poor man's house, it must be taken care of, and cannot be boarded out, as it would be by gentlefolks, or sent to a public or private asylum for such unfortunate beings. [Poor people,] seeing frequently among their neighbours such objects, easily [forget] whatever there is of natural disgust about them, and have [therefore] a sane state, so that without pain or suffering they [perform] their duties towards them.*

After referring to an idiot who lives within a mile of his own house who is remarkably '*handsome in ... person and features*' Wordsworth points out:

> *It is not enough for me as a Poet, to delineate merely such feelings as all men do sympathize with; but it is highly*

> *desirable to add to these others, such as all men* may
> *sympathize with, and such as there is reason to believe they*
> *would be better and more moral beings if they did*
> *sympathise with.*

The moral and didactic purpose of the poem is clear here but
it is a didacticism quite different from that to which Keats
objects in the later poetry, that which has a *'palpable design upon
us'*. Here the moral is conveyed through the fable; the plight of
the distraught mother is strongly and effectively shown, the
indifference of the Doctor a concrete condemnation of the
sophistication of the town that cannot see the needs of 'poor
people' who cannot express themselves effectively. The in-
articulateness of Johnny is mirrored in that of his mother, her
simplicity matches his and that of the poet in telling his story.
And behind this social and moral comment also lies another: a
theme that is the constantly recurring one in the early
Wordsworth. This is an awareness of an order in Nature within
which Betty Foy, Johnny and Susan Gale belong, and which
serves as a background for the poem. The moonlight is a
constant feature in the poem, and the passage of the night and
the growing anxiety of the mother as her son does not return is
vividly presented. The poem is full of detailed psychological
observation seen, for example, in the change of attitude of the
mother, at first angry with her son for his seeming dilatoriness:

> *The clock is on the stroke of twelve,*
> *And Johnny is not yet in sight :*
> *— The Moon's in heaven, as Betty sees,*
> *But Betty is not quite at ease ;*
> *And Susan has a dreadful night.*
>
> *And Betty, half an hour ago,*
> *On Johnny vile reflections cast :*
> *'A little idle sauntering Thing !'*
> *With other names, an endless string ;*
> *But now that time is gone and past.*[3]

to her powerfully sustained relief when she is reunited with
Johnny again:

> *And now she's at the Pony's tail,*
> *And now is at the Pony's head, —*
> *On that side now, and now on this ;*

And, almost stifled with her bliss,
A few sad tears does Betty shed.

She kisses o'er and o'er again
Him whom she loves, her Idiot Boy;
She's happy here, is happy there,
She is uneasy every where;
Her limbs are all alive with joy ...

'Oh! Johnny, never mind the Doctor;
You've done your best, and that is all:'
She took the reins, when this was said,
And gently turned the Pony's head
From the loud waterfall.[4]

The closeness of the observation here, the strong and powerful feeling that is conveyed through the seemingly artless simplicity of the lines is astonishingly effective and the only barrier to our reading the poem with enjoyment and understanding is an inability to attend to it because of a preconception about Wordsworth's poetry of this period. We must not confuse the language of his characters with that of the poet himself; as an observer of humanity he is allowing us to share with him the insights into human nature that he can achieve through a fable of this kind. In this technique, Wordsworth is genuinely building upon the strengths of the original ballad tradition and he is pointing forward to the way in which simple folk are to be used as repositories of strong moral awareness in the nineteenth century novel, in such writers as Dickens and Hardy, who also draw much of their strength from the same ballad tradition. The path that begins with Wordsworth's *Idiot Boy* is the one that ends with Hardy's *Ruined Maid*, the same 'artlessness' is at work in the best ballad writings of both poets.

It would be idle to pretend that the whole of the *Lyrical Ballads* is successful in this way. By no means all the poems, even of the first edition, are in any sense 'ballads', and those that are not are, on the whole, much less successful. There was always in Wordsworth two contrary tendencies at work: on the one hand there was the acute and sympathetic observer of human affairs as we have just been glancing at; on the other, there was the moralizing preacher who became far too predominant in the later years. In the chance remark quoted from the letter to John

A Lakeland scene (Esmor Jones)

Wilson that there was an 'idiot' not a mile from where he lived, Wordsworth gives us a clue to the origin of his best work. When this was located in the realities of directly observed experience he was always at his best. When the writing was located, instead, in meditation upon that experience in more abstract terms he was often at his most limited. There are in *Lyrical Ballads* a number of poems that are more explicitly concerned with philosophical or psychological ideas and these are much less successful. In spite of Coleridge's constant insistence upon his ability to write a great philosophical poem, few poets have ever been less well equipped for this and the tragedy of Wordsworth is the way in which the lesser side of his talent gradually takes over from the genuine inspiration of the earlier poems.

A good example of this tendency at work, even in the 1798 volume, can be seen in the two poems *Expostulation and Reply* and *The Tables Turned: an Evening Scene, on the same subject.* In these much anthologized poems, Wordsworth is talking about the nature of wisdom with his schoolmaster friend, Matthew, and argues the case for learning from Nature rather than from books. There is some biographical evidence for supposing that the poems represent Wordsworth's own way of life: his servant was accustomed to telling visitors that his study was out-of-doors rather than the room in which he kept his books so Matthew's 'expostulation' that he should not be:

'... on that old grey stone,
thus for the length of half a day,

Why, William, sit you thus alone,
And dream your time away?'

makes sense in terms of his own method of working. Wordsworth's reply summarizes his view of poetic inspiration and is along much the same lines as the second version of the Preface, but the poem as a whole fails to convince at any other than an intellectual level.

It is difficult to come to the *Lyrical Ballads* with a genuine sense of freshness. If we succeed in doing so, however, if we can read them as skilful and wholly original manipulators of the art of the dramatic monologue, we shall come close to some understanding of where the real strengths of these poems lay. We may also understand something of Wordsworth's own disappointment at their apparent rejection by those whom he might most have expected to understand him. Of modern critics, it is essentially Helen Darbishire in *The Poet Wordsworth*[5] and John Danby in *The Simple Wordsworth*[6] who have come closest to an appreciation of the spirit in which these remarkable poems are written. It is through a stripping of both poetry and mankind to their simplest, through an exploration of Nature and mankind fused together in a harmony and put into a concrete situation that Wordsworth achieves his effect. As Helen Darbishire puts it in writing of *The Thorn*: *'We see the wild desolate scene* through *the human passion, whilst the stark human passions are lifted into permanence, even beauty, by the setting of earth, air and sky.'*

In poetry of this kind, and in a few of the poems included in the second edition, especially the *Lucy* sequence, Wordsworth achieves a Shakespearean power to comprehend humanity within the simplicity of the setting he gives it. Later he was to go to do other, and different, things, but he never again attempted, or achieved, the particular achievement of the best of the *Lyrical Ballads*. They may have been in a sense, as we have seen, of their time, but they also transcended it. As Jones and Tydeman[7] summarize it: *'The "experiment" to which he refers in the Advertisement of 1798 had been completed and was never repeated.'*

[1] William Wordsworth *The Idiot Boy* stanzas 50–2 [2] *ibid.* stanza 63 [3] *ibid.* stanzas 31–2 [4] *ibid.* stanzas 77–80 [5] Helen Darbishire *The Poet Wordsworth* (O.U.P., 1950) [6] J. F. Danby *The Simple Wordsworth* (Routledge & Kegan Paul, 1960) [7] A. C. Jones and W. Tydeman (eds) *Wordsworth: Lyrical Ballads* (Macmillan 'Casebook' series, 1972)

6

The Prelude

Wordsworth's first biographer wrote of him: '*He wrote as he lived, and he lived as he wrote. His poetry had its heart in his life, and his life found a voice in his poetry.*' This chapter is necessarily complementary to the first one. There it was impossible to describe the nature of Wordsworth's life without reference to *The Prelude*; here it will be necessary again and again to refer to biographical facts in discussing the long poem which was always spoken of by him as '*the Poem of my own life*'. A book such as this cannot do more than present the most elementary introduction to a reading of *The Prelude*. For adequate critical comment the reader must be referred to other sources but there are a number of obstacles that need clearing out of the way before any reading of *The Prelude* can be undertaken. That is the primary purpose of the present chapter.

The first necessity is to be aware of the kind of poem that it is, both in intention and in actual outcome. As the title suggests, *The Prelude* was never intended to stand by itself but was a starting point for an even longer and more ambitious poem that Wordsworth had long had the intention of writing. This was to have been called *The Recluse* and one of the earliest references to it is in a letter of Wordsworth's to James Tobin of 6th March, 1798: '*I have written 1300 lines of a poem in which I contrive to convey most of the knowledge of which I am possessed. My object is to give pictures of Nature, Man and Society ... The work of composition is carved out for me, for at least a year and a half to come.*' From then on, there are frequent references in the private writings of the Wordsworth circle to this major poem, in the task of composing which he was greatly and continuously encouraged by Coleridge in the years of their intimate friendship. This was to have been the most important poem that could be composed and one for which, in Coleridge's view, Wordsworth was uniquely suited. In a letter to the Member of Parliament,

Richard Sharp, in 1804, Coleridge makes the point that he was to make over and over again to correspondents and to Wordsworth himself:

> *Wordsworth is a poet, a most original poet. He no more resembles Milton than Milton resembles Shakespeare — no more resembles Shakespeare than Shakespeare resembles Milton. He is himself and, I dare affirm that, he will hereafter be admitted as the first and greatest philosophical poet, the only man who has effected a complete and constant synthesis of thought and feeling and combined them with poetic forms, with the music of pleasurable passion, and with Imagination or the* modifying *power in the highest sense of that word, in which I have ventured to oppose it to Fancy, or the aggregating power — in that sense in which it is a dim analogue of creation — not all that we can* believe, *but all that we can* conceive *of creation.*

It will be seen, therefore, that this poem dealing with 'Nature, Man and Society', as it is constantly spoken of, was to be a most ambitious project. The purpose of *The Prelude* was to introduce it, to show, in fact, how Wordsworth had become fitted and prepared to undertake this task. *The Recluse* was to be one of the major philosophical poems of all time, to take its place in the long line of epic works from Virgil to Milton, and, as we shall see, his illustrious predecessors, especially Milton, were very much in Wordsworth's mind in undertaking the work. The task, in the end, proved too daunting and the later references to it have a note of sadness in comparison with the ambitious notes at the beginning of the undertaking. In April 1822, Wordsworth is writing to Landor: 'The Recluse *has had a long sleep, save in my thoughts; my mss. are so ill-penned and blurred that they are useless to all but myself; and at present I cannot face them,*' and in 1841 one of the last references to the project has a note of finality in a letter from Aubrey de Vere to his sister: '*Wordsworth says* The Recluse *has never been written except a few passages — and probably never will . . .*'

What, then, went wrong, and what was the writing history of this huge project to which we owe, in spite of its lack of completion, not only *The Prelude* but much else of the longer poetry of Wordsworth? It will be helpful to try to get the chronology right from the start.

The starting point was almost certainly the composition of *The Ruined Cottage* in 1797–8. This was a narrative by a pedlar and, as an addendum, Wordsworth included an account of the narrator's mind. The plan here was very similar to that later adopted for *The Prelude* in the idea that to understand a narrative poem we need also to understand something of the character of the teller of the story. However, although we may discern some resemblances between the poet and the pedlar in *The Ruined Cottage*, the identification is by no means complete and the use of dramatic narration gives added opportunities for irony and comment by the poet himself. We know from *Lyrical Ballads* and the use here of dramatic monologue as one of the narrative techniques that Wordsworth was particularly interested in this method of telling a tale at this time (he was, of course, also experimenting with drama proper in *The Borderers*), and it is worth reading the finally published version of *The Ruined Cottage* with this in mind. The final version was eventually published as the first book of *The Excursion* in 1814 in which on '*a summer forenoon the Author reaches a ruined cottage upon a Common, and there meets with a revered friend, the Wanderer of whose education and course of life he gives an account.*' Certain other poems, that were later to be incorporated into *The Prelude*, also date from the 1798 period, notably the meeting with the Old Soldier that now forms the conclusion to Book IV. This, together with a number of other passages, was originally composed as a separate poem and only incorporated into the grand design later.

By now, towards the end of 1798, Wordsworth and Coleridge had begun to conceive the idea of the great philosophical poem to be entitled 'The Recluse' and reference to it becomes frequent in their letters and other writings. The following year, 1799, Wordsworth spent the winter in Germany and while there he began to draft the passages of autobiography dealing with his childhood which later appeared in *The Prelude*.

In 1800 Wordsworth wrote *Home at Grasmere*, which was to have been the first book of *The Recluse* proper. This received eventual publication, as *The Recluse* in 1888, but the closing lines had been published as a 'prospectus' to *The Excursion* in 1814. This makes clear what the scope of the project is now, as Wordsworth conceives it:

> *On Man, on Nature, and on Human Life*
> *Musing in Solitude, I oft perceive*

Fair trains of imagery before me rise,
Accompanied by feelings of delight
Pure, or with no unpleasing sadness mixed,
And I am conscious of affecting thoughts
And dear remembrances, whose presence soothes
Or elevates the Mind, intent to weigh
The good and evil of our mortal state.[1]

Certainly by now Wordsworth saw his poetry as forming a potential unity which would be provided by *The Recluse*. The Preface of 1814 to *The Excursion* somewhat labours the point:

Several years ago, when the Author retired to his native mountains, with the hope of being able to construct a literary Work that might live, it was a reasonable thing that he should take a review of his own mind, and examine how far Nature and Education had qualified him for such employment. As subsidiary to this preparation, he undertook to record, in verse, the origin and progress of his own powers, as far as he was acquainted with them. That Work, addressed to a dear Friend, most distinguished for his knowledge and genius, and to whom the Author's Intellect is deeply indebted, has been long finished ; and the result of the investigation which gave rise to it was a determination to compose a philosophical poem, containing views of Man, Nature, and Society ; and to be entitled, 'The Recluse'; as having for its principal subject the sensations and opinions of a poet living in retirement. The preparatory poem is biographical, and conducts the history of the Author's mind to the point when he was emboldened to hope that his faculties were sufficiently matured for entering upon the arduous labour which he had proposed to himself; and the two Works have the same kind of relation to each other, if he may so express himself, as the ante-chapel has to the body of a gothic church. Continuing this allusion, he may be permitted to add, that his minor Pieces, which have been long before the Public, when they shall be properly arranged, will be found by the attentive Reader to have such connection with the main Work as may give them claim to be likened to the little cells, oratories, and sepulchral recesses, ordinarily included in those edifices.

Thus the poem was now to consist of three parts: *The Prelude* as we know it; *The Excursion* in which '*something of a dramatic form*

[is] *adopted*'; and *The Recluse* which will '*consist chiefly of meditations in the Author's own person*'. The evidence of the letters makes it clear that something like this as a total design had begun to take shape in Wordsworth's mind as early as 1804. At any rate by 1805, *The Pedlar*, the addendum to *The Ruined Cottage*, had been completed and so had the first version of *The Prelude*. In 1814, as we have seen, *The Excursion* was published to a variety of critical responses which we examine in Chapter 8. From then on, Wordsworth spent many years revising *The Prelude* and he seems to have completed the revisions to produce the poem in something like its final form by 1839. It was still to await the conclusion of *The Recluse* before it was published, however, and, as we have seen, that poem never was written and was eventually abandoned by about 1841. Nine years later, after Wordsworth's death in 1850, *The Prelude*, in what was substantially its 1839 version, was published posthumously when it had, of course, to compete for interest with that other great, long Victorian poem, Tennyson's *In Memoriam*. If *The Prelude* attracted relatively little serious critical attention at that time, it was because it was really a poem that belonged to an earlier age. Only on publication of the 1805 version by Professor de Selincourt in 1926, in an edition which set the 1805 and the 1850 texts alongside each other, did the poem's real nature begin to emerge.

The chronology is complex but has had to be explored because our reading of *The Prelude* is enhanced by an awareness of where it was intended to stand within the total scheme of the poet's intentions and by a realization of the differences between the two versions. Certainly, even so shrewd a judge as Macaulay was misled by the nature of the publication history of the poem to see it in a light that some critics have seen it in ever since:

> *I brought home, and read,* The Prelude. *It is a poorer* Excursion; *the same sort of faults and beauties, but the faults greater, and the beauties fainter, both in themselves, and because faults are always made more oppressive, and beauties less pleasing, by repetition. The story is the old story. There are the old raptures about mountains and cataracts; the old flimsy philosophy about the effect of scenery on the mind; the old crazy mystical metaphysics, the endless wildernesses of dull, flat prosaic twaddle; and here and there fine descriptions and energetic declamations interspersed.*[2]

Everyone knows, and most would admire, some of the great set passages from *The Prelude*: the stolen boat episode, the skating on the ice, and so on. Certainly one would not wish to deny the greatness of these passages but they can only be seen rightfully within the context of the long biographical poem as a whole. We cannot, without doing violence to both the intention and achievement of the author, take out those bits of *The Prelude* that happen to appeal to us because they look like something that we can recognize as poetry and leave the rest.

2

I have already made clear my preference for the earlier version of the poem. It is a pity that in most standard editions of Wordsworth it is still the 1850 text that is commonly printed and consequently this is the one with which most readers are familiar. Not all critics would agree with this view. Even so perceptive a critic as John Speirs, writing in *Poetry towards Novel*,[3] explaining his reasons for generally quoting from the 1850 version writes:

> *Wordsworth tended not to alter his best passages much. They are substantially there from the beginning. The 1805 version is more of an effusion, in that sense 'fresher' and more immediate in places. But the final text ... seems to me on the whole the best to read. Most of the alterations made over many years are stylistic only (but in the best sense), most are improvements, some not.*

The only way to examine a statement of this kind is by a detailed process of comparison between the two versions and to do this with a few selected passages is a valuable exercise in criticism. For a helpful exploration of the issues raised by the variant readings the best source of help and comment is still the review by Helen Darbishire of de Selincourt's 1926 comparative edition, reprinted in McMaster.[4]

For our purposes it is enough to note now the diminished psychological effectiveness and truth of the later version, and presently to explore the way in which what had begun as a genuine work of philosophical exploration in the earlier version, becomes a collection of conventional pieties by the time it was published in 1850. Small wonder, then, that in the context of its time it was little understood and vastly under-rated.

Coleridge, of course, was a surer critic than most others when it came to dealing with these matters. On the memorable occasion of Wordsworth's reading to him the original version of *The Prelude* in 1807, he wrote a poem addressed to Wordsworth which ends with a fitting and moving tribute:

> *And when—O Friend my comforter and guide*
> *Strong in thyself, and powerful to give strength—*
> *Thy long sustained Song finally closed,*
> *And thy deep voice had ceased—yet thou thyself*
> *Wert still before my eyes, and round us both*
> *That happy vision of beloved faces—*
> *Scarce conscious, and yet conscious of its close*
> *I state, my being blended in one thought*
> *(Thought was it? or aspiration? or resolve?)*
> *Absorbed, yet hanging still upon the sound—*
> *And when I rose, I found myself in prayer.*

It is a moment of rare intimacy that we are allowed to share between two of the masterminds of their age.

Later, in May 1815, after Coleridge had written to Lady Beaumont to express disappointment with *The Excursion*, Wordsworth wrote a little petulantly, asking him to explain '*where I have failed*'. Coleridge replied:

> *In order, therefore, to explain the* disappointment *I must recall to your mind what my* expectations *were: and, as these again were founded on the supposition that (in whatever order it might be published) the poem on the growth of your own mind was as the ground plot and roots, out of which 'The Recluse' was to have sprung up as the tree, as far as (there was) the same sap in both, I expected them doubtless, to have formed one complete whole; but in matter, form, and product to be different, each not only distinct but a different work ... I ... anticipated as commencing with you set down and settled in an abiding home, and that with the description of that home you were to begin a* philosophical poem, *the* result *and fruits of a spirit so framed and so disciplined as had been told in the former.*

In the event, as we have seen, the much hoped for and anticipated 'philosophical' poem in *The Recluse* never appeared and we must accept that the poem of the kind that Coleridge so consistently wanted him to produce was not the kind of poem Wordsworth was best able to produce. His own instinct was probably right when he delayed its writing for so long. But Coleridge, who had the advantage over Macaulay of hearing the original version, was right to prefer *The Prelude* to *The Excursion*. Properly understood it was, in fact, the very poem for which he was seeking and which he had been urging Wordsworth to produce over so many years, and it is to the status and nature of *The Prelude* as a poetical exploration in philosophy and psychology that we must now turn our consideration.

It is hardly surprising that with so long a poem composed over so long a period there is sufficient evidence for any number of conflicting critical interpretations. No attempt is likely to be successful that wrenches a philosophical 'message' out of the poem. *The Prelude*, like any other great, long poem, is its own statement; it is emphatically not the versifying of an already existing philosophy. Certainly one of its key themes is how man may regain an innocent paradise that he once inhabited in childhood through the developed power of the Imagination and through the intercourse with Nature that the Imagination makes possible. At the beginning of *The Prelude* Wordsworth recalls the innocence of the world of childhood:

> *Oh, many a time have I, a five years' child,*
> *In a small mill-race severed from his stream,*
> *Made one long bathing of a summer's day;*
> *Basked in the sun, and plunged and basked again*
> *Alternate, all a summer's day ...*
> *   as if I had been born*
> *On Indian plains, and from my mother's hut*
> *Had run abroad in wantonness, to sport,*
> *A naked savage, in the thunder shower.*[5]

Later he tells us the significance of recollections like these:

> *There are in our existence spots of time,*
> *That with distinct pre-eminence retain*
> *A renovating virtue, whence, depressed*
> *By false opinion and contentious thought,*
> *Or aught of heavier or more deadly weight,*
> *In trivial occupations, and the round*
> *Of ordinary intercourse, our minds*
> *Are nourished and invisibly repaired ...*

> *Such moments*
> *Are scattered everywhere, taking their date*
> *From our first childhood.*[6]

Specifically, Wordsworth goes on to recall in Book XII how as a child he had come across a place where a gibbet had once stood and where the name of a hanged man was carved into the rock. Such a moment and the thoughts it led to transformed the rest of the ordinary scene and landscape:

> *A casual glance had shown them, and I fled,*
> *Faltering and faint, and ignorant of the road:*
> *Then, reascending the bare common, saw*
> *A naked pool that lay beneath the hills,*
> *The beacon on the summit, and, more near,*
> *A girl, who bore a pitcher on her head,*
> *And seemed with difficult steps to force her way*
> *Against the blowing wind. It was, in truth,*
> *An ordinary sight; but I should need*
> *Colours and words that are unknown to man,*
> *To paint the visionary dreariness*
> *Which, while I looked all round for my lost guide,*
> *Invested moorland waste, and naked pool,*
> *The beacon crowning the low eminence,*
> *The female and her garments vexed and tossed*
> *By the strong wind.*[7]

Several aspects of this passage are typical of one important element of *The Prelude*. Above all, there is the sharpness of observation and the almost total recall of the experience. It was not just the carved letters with their grim background that were remembered in the scene, though they gave it its first significance. But, in remembering them, all the attendant circumstances are also recalled, even to the way in which the girl walked buffetted by the wind. Yet for anyone else: '*It was, in truth an ordinary sight*'. The sights which Wordsworth saw, anyone might have seen, the experiences that he had and recalls in *The Prelude* were in no way out-of-the-ordinary experiences. They are, in fact, the common experiences of mankind, the Poet '*is a man speaking to men*' in *The Prelude* as much as anywhere else. But he is a man endowed with a particular sensibility which enables him to see the ordinary in different terms to that of other men, his powers are normal human powers but tuned to a degree that all men have not so far possessed themselves of. The journey which Wordsworth describes in *The Prelude* of his own life is essentially not being claimed as a unique one. He stands here for all mankind, the odyssey on which he travels is one for all mankind to travel with him. To write a poem of this kind in any other way would have been the utmost in arrogance and egoism; *The Prelude* is of value not just as the record of the life experience of one man but as being typical of the experience of mankind as a whole. Wordsworth himself may be the centre of the poem but its theme, nonetheless, is Man.

This means that we cannot really read the poem as a piece of pure autobiography. Many important aspects of the actual life of Wordsworth are omitted or passed over very lightly, in some cases for obvious reasons, as in the Annette Vallon incident, for example. But this does not invalidate *The Prelude* as a poem that seeks to explore the nature of the growth of the human mind in a self-conscious awareness of what had been taken for granted in the innocence of early childhood. The poem is one of spiritual growth and restoration; the last thing that ought to be said of *The Prelude* is that it is escapist literature, seeking comfort and solace in the countryside for a world that has become wearisome in its emphasis on towns and material values.

The starting point is made quite explicit in the echoes of Milton with which *The Prelude* begins. Not only is Wordsworth here staking his claim artistically to be linked with his illustrious predecessor but he is also marking out the nature of his theme. *Paradise Lost* ends with the founders of the human race being expelled from Eden:

> *The world was all before them, where to choose,*
> *Their place of rest, and Providence their guide.*

Wordsworth takes up the story where Milton had left off:

> *The earth is all before me. With a heart*
> *Joyous, nor scared at its own liberty,*
> *I look about ; and should the chosen guide*
> *Be nothing better than a wandering cloud,*
> *I cannot miss my way.*[8]

His theme, at this level, is to be man's search for, and regaining of, Paradise. The guide that Providence has provided is to be found in Nature, but not only in her soothing qualities alone. The famous passage about the stolen boat in Book I shows

that even in earliest childhood, Nature could have a menacing as
well as a welcome aspect and that we would find in her what we
deserved to find. Yet, for all the menace of this passage and the
sense of almost supernatural dread that it conveys:

> *and when the deed was done*
> *I heard among the solitary hills*
> *Low breathings coming after me, and sounds*
> *Of undistinguishable motion, steps*
> *Almost as silent as the turf they trod.*[9]

The whole incident is perfectly explicable in naturalistic terms as
an effect of the perspective, the huge hill that 'upreared its head'
has simply been revealed from behind the hill that had
previously hidden it as 'the horizon's bound'. Once again it is a
perfectly ordinary event, one to be discerned daily and nightly in
the Lake District, but invested with a special power by the effect
of the Imagination which transforms it into an extraordinary
event from which Man can learn as he reflects upon the
experience afterwards:

> *after I had seen*
> *The spectacle, for many days, my brain*
> *Worked with a dim and undetermined sense*
> *Of unknown modes of being.*[10]

The main point is that there is nothing that is without
meaning and significance: the whole world of Nature is a parable
written large from which we are capable of learning if we have
eyes to see and ears to hear. The two poems, *Expostulation and
Reply* and *The Tables Turned* had already made this point; *The
Prelude* is a more successful elaboration in poetic terms of the
ideas contained there. It is a triumphant demonstration of *how*:

> *One impulse from a vernal wood*
> *May teach you more of man,*
> *Of moral evil and of good,*
> *Than all the sages can.*[11]

As a bare statement of fact this fails to convince; in *The Prelude*
we see this conviction, which for Wordsworth was a statement of
plain fact, powerfully vindicated.

It is important to recognize that *The Prelude* is, like its
predecessor, *Paradise Lost*, intended as one of the great
synthesizing achievements of the human intellect. It was not for

The statue of Newton in Trinity College, Cambridge (Kate Grillet)

nothing that Wordsworth had gone to Cambridge to study mathematics and that he recalled Newton's statue in Trinity College chapel:

> *And from my pillow, looking forth by light*
> *Of moon or favouring stars, I could behold*
> *The antechapel where the statue stood*
> *Of Newton with his prism and silent face,*
> *The marble index of a mind for ever*
> *Voyaging through strange seas of Thought, alone.*[12]

The placing of that last word 'alone' is masterly: it conveys the loneliness and isolation that must be endured by those strong enough to engage themselves with the task of increasing the span of human knowledge. Newton had brought about a synthesis of the known facts about the physical universe; his was essentially a work of the creative Imagination—even the story about the fall of the apple is not unlike the moments of revelation that Wordsworth described in 'the spots of time' passages in *The Prelude*. Wordsworth's own task is to take this further, to explore the inner and spiritual world as Newton had explored the outer and physical one, to bring about a synthesis through which mankind may be restored to Paradise:

> *I looked for universal things; perused*
> *The common countenance of earth and sky:*
> *Earth, nowhere unembellished by some trace*
> *Of that first paradise whence man was driven;*
> *And sky, whose beauty and bounty are expressed*
> *By the proud name she bears—the name of Heaven.*
> *I called on both to teach me what they might;*
> *Or turning the mind in upon herself*
> *Pored, watched, expected, listened, spread my thoughts*
> *And spread them with a wider creeping; felt*
> *Incumbencies more awful, visitings*
> *Of the Upholder of the tranquil soul,*
> *That tolerates the indignities of Time,*
> *And, from the centre of Eternity*
> *All finite motions overruling, lives*
> *In glory immutable.*[13]

Newton had had to conduct his voyage through the seas of thought alone; he can now act as our guide in matters of the intellect later. Wordsworth, in his quest, too, has to journey for much of the time alone.

Those who think of him only as an escapist writer living surrounded by streams and trees and hills should read this corrosive attack upon a city that is the embodiment of evil because there is in it no order, no acceptance of any system of values that can give a worthwhile currency to what is seen and done. In this 'monstrous ant-hill' the fine and the trivial are incongruously mingled together: even the busts and statues present alongside each other:

> *Boyle, Shakespeare, Newton, or the attractive head*
> *Of some quack-doctor, famous in his day.*[14]

The city is in fact a gigantic and monstrous 'masquerade' where the imitations of humanity rather than humanity itself abide. Nothing could be further removed from the sonnet on Westminster Bridge; here in Book VII of *The Prelude* we are much closer to Blake's *London* and to the world of 'the infant harlot's cry'. It is a further mark of the selectivity of much of our reading of Wordsworth that passages of this quality, which are far removed from the conventional picture we have formed of him, do not spring easily to the mind in thinking about his poetry.

In the use of the city in *The Prelude*, Wordsworth gives a further demonstration of the poem's modernity. The very things that both the attackers and defenders of city life have pointed to in our own time find their place here.

> *Private courts,*
> *Gloomy as coffins, and unsightly lanes*
> *Thrilled by some female vendor's scream, belike*
> *The very shrillest of all London cries,*
> *May then entangle our impatient steps;*
> *Conducted through those labyrinths, unawares,*
> *To privileged regions and inviolate,*
> *Where from their airy lodges studious lawyers*
> *Look out on waters, walks, and gardens green.*[15]

A passage such as this needs to be set alongside some of the more outspoken passages on the French Revolution in Book IX to make its full impact. London, like France, was, of course, filled with beggars, who again speak to Wordsworth through the eyes and ears of the Imagination:

> *Amid the moving pageant, I was smitten*
> *Abruptly, with the view (a sight not rare)*
> *Of a blind Beggar, who, with upright face,*
> *Stood, propped against a wall, upon his chest*
> *Wearing a written paper, to explain*
> *His story, whence he came, and who he was.*
> *Caught by the spectacle my mind turned round*
> *As with the might of waters; an apt type*
> *This label seemed of the utmost we can know,*
> *Both of ourselves and of the universe;*
> *And, on the shape of that unmoving man,*
> *His steadfast face and sightless eyes, I gazed,*
> *As if admonished from another world.*[16]

At one level, of course, this beggar makes us think ahead to Beaupuy's statement in Book IX: *''Tis against* that *that we are fighting'* (Wordsworth's emphasis), but he should also recall for us the proud peasant-stock of Cumberland, perhaps above all the leech-gatherer in *Resolution and Independence*. The whole of Book VII is filled with images that have their answer and antidote elsewhere in *The Prelude* and in the rest of Wordsworth's work. There is even the boy being initiated into corruption early in his infancy to be compared with the infancy and childhood of

Wordsworth and his companions dealt with in the first Books. The London book comes, rightly, at the centre of *The Prelude* and upon its power and success we may rightly claim that Wordsworth is the first modern poet of urban life. It is a valuable corrective to the received view of Wordsworth as the poet who simply celebrated the simplicity of 'humble and rustic life'.

3

There is clearly no space in an introductory book for a full analysis of *The Prelude*. Enough has probably been said to give some conception of its ambitious nature and some further aspects of its thought will be examined in Chapter 8. But it would be wrong to leave the poem without reference to one other aspect that has only been touched on so far and that is its concern with the detailed exploration of individual psychology; its interest in the very processes by which the human mind operates. In this *The Prelude* emerges as a very modern poem also; indeed John Speirs in *Poetry towards Novel* stresses the way in which it anticipates the distinctive subject-matter of the Victorian novel and the obsession there with the theme of children growing up, to discover the ways in which the child proves the father of the man. Certainly it is difficult to think of an earlier work in which there is so comprehensive a treatment of this topic, one which probably would not have been thought of as significant before the time of Rousseau in any case. *The Prelude* is an important turning point in our consideration of the role of the child in literature. As Speirs puts it:

> *The nearest parallel is, perhaps, the fullness and richness of George Eliot's recollections of the provincial English life of the Warwickshire of her childhood and youth out of which she began making her novels when, at the age of forty, detached now by time and place ... she discovered herself as a novelist. In the poetry of Wordsworth, as in the novels of George Eliot and Dickens, these memories of childhood and youth flow back into the consciousness with unusual distinctness and abundance. But, though recollected experiences form the substance of the poetry of* The Prelude *(as of the novels of George Eliot) it is what is made of that substance that is the poetry (or that is the novel) ... The poet himself is necessarily in many ways no longer the same*

person as the child or youth to whom these things originally happened. He is and he is not the same, though he recognizes that he is the kind of man he now is partly as a result of those childhood and boyhood experiences.[17]

In this reflection from a standpoint of maturity upon the experiences of the past Wordsworth is engaging in a new kind of psychological exploration.

Enough has been said to establish that if we are to read *The Prelude* at all, we must read it with care and attention and we must read it as a whole. It is insufficient and unfair to its author to extract from *The Prelude* the 'purple passages' of 'poetry' and to suppose that in having read those we have read all that matters. The philosophy and the pyschology of *The Prelude* are inseparable from the poem as a whole. Of course it does have its moments of longeurs, it is probably impossible to write a poem of extended length in which this is not the case, but they, too, moments of rest within the total fabric and orchestration of the poem, are part of the whole design. We are not used, today, to poems of this kind of extended length, nor are we used to poetry that attempts so much as *The Prelude*. We no longer turn to poetry for enlightenment on matters of moral philosophy and psychology. In that sense we have to make an effort of the historical imagination to cope with a reading of *The Prelude*, as we do in reading *The Canterbury Tales*, or *The Divine Comedy*, or *Paradise Lost*. But, like all those works, and many others that belong to the same literary traditions, it is essentially of its own time and essentially of ours also. If we are looking for the definitive start of the 'modern poem' *The Prelude* is as good a beginning as any.

[1] William Wordsworth *Home at Grasmere* ll 754–62 [2] G. O. Trevelyan *The Life and Letters of Lord Macaulay* (Longman, 1876) [3] John Speirs *Poetry towards Novel* (Faber & Faber, 1971) [4] Graham McMaster (ed.) *Penguin Critical Anthology of Criticism on Wordsworth* (Penguin, 1972) [5] William Wordsworth *The Prelude* (1850 version) Bk I ll 288–300 [6] *ibid.* Bk XII ll 208–25 [7] *ibid.* Bk XII ll 246–61 [8] *ibid.* Bk I ll 14–18 [9] *ibid.* Bk I ll 321–5 [10] *ibid.* Bk I ll 390–3 [11] William Wordsworth *The Tables Turned* ll 21–4 [12] As 5 (1850 version) Bk III ll 58–63 [13] *ibid.* Bk III ll 109–24 [14] *ibid.* Bk VII ll 166–7 [15] *ibid.* Bk VII ll 180–8 [16] *ibid.* Bk VII ll 637–49 [17] As 3 p. 83

7

The Wordsworth Circle

Long before he became settled in fame at Rydal Mount,
Wordsworth had a wide circle of literary friends, many of whom
are worth a book in their own right. Even though there never was
in reality what its detractors tended to speak of as a 'Lake school
of poetry', Dove Cottage was a place to which many of the
writers of the time made their way and in some cases they made
it their home also. Alongside this, we must place Wordsworth's
own frequent trips away from the Lakes to visit other parts of the
country to maintain his contacts with contemporary writers.
Although he may have been a man who preferred to be alone
while actually composing his works, Wordsworth was in no sense
a solitary figure and the roll of those whom he knew in the literary
establishment of his day is a most impressive one.

First amongst these must, of course, come the two who were
closest to him and who shared so much of his life in the Lakes,
his sister, Dorothy, and Coleridge. It was his good fortune to
spend much of his life surrounded by adoring women who
sought nothing better than to look after him and to give him time
to write his poems. Something of his relationship with his sister
has already been explored but her own skill as a writer and as a
recorder of the passing scene in her *Journals* needs yet further
emphasis. In Chapter 3 we have seen how much her perceptions
of natural beauty affected his own, and her *Journals* are a source
of constant delight in the natural beauty that she records. Along
with this goes the vivid picture that emerges of their life together
at Grasmere, a life filled with small incidents of pleasure but one
also not without its daily toils. Here are some entries for 1800:

> Sunday Morning, 3rd August. *I made pies and stuffed the
> pike—baked a loaf. Headache after dinner—I lay down. A
> letter from Wm rouzed me, desiring us to go to Keswick.
> After writing to Wm we walked as far as Mr Simpson's*

and ate black cherries. A Heavenly warm evening with scattered clouds upon the hills. There was a vernal greeness upon the grass from the rains of the morning and afternoon. Peas for dinner.

Monday 4th. *Rain in the night. I tied up Scarlet beans, nailed the honeysuckles etc. etc. John was prepared to walk to Keswick all the morning. He seized a returned chaise and went after dinner. I pulled a large basket of peas and sent to Keswick by a returned chaise. A very cold evening. Assisted to spread out linen in the morning.*

Wednesday 6th August. *A rainy morning. I ironed till dinner time—sewed till near dark—then pulled a basket of peas, and afterwards boiled and picked gooseberries. William came home from Keswick at 11 o'clock. A very fine night.*

Thursday Morning, 7th August. *Packed up the mattrass, and sent to Keswick. Boiled gooseberries—N.B. 2 lbs of sugar in the first panfull, 3 quarts all good measure—3 lbs in the 2nd 4 quarts—2½ lbs in the 3rd. A very fine day. William composing in the wood in the morning. In the evening we walked to Mary Point. A very fine sunset.*

Sunday 12th October. *Beautiful day. Sate in the house writing in the morning while Wm went into the Wood to compose. Wrote to John in the morning—copied poems for the L(yrical) B(allads), in the evening wrote to Mrs Rawson. Mary Jameson and Sally Ashburner dined. We pulled apples after dinner, a large basket full. We walked before tea by Bainriggs to observe the many coloured foliage the oaks dark green with yellow leaves, the birches generally still green, some near the water yellowish. The Sycamore crimson and crimson-tufted, the mountain ash a deep orange, the common ash Lemon colour but many ashes still fresh in their summer green. Those that were discoloured chiefly near the water. William composing in the Evening. Went to bed at 12 o'clock.*

It is an honest and appealing picture that is given of the frugal and skilled housekeeper making the best she could of the fruit

Dorothy Wordsworth
from an oil painting by
Samuel Crosthwaite
(Reproduced by
courtesy of Mr
Richard Wordsworth)

Portrait of Coleridge
by Vandyke (National
Portrait Gallery,
London)

and vegetables that they had in the garden, copying out her brother's poems in their final versions, making nature observations, and generally busying herself with her daily, and often mundane, tasks. The *Journals* are essential reading for anyone who wants to know the quality of life in the Wordsworth household and amongst their pleasures is the series of candid and odd glimpses they give us of the literary figures of the day seen through Dorothy's unromanticizing eye.

Amongst these was Coleridge, whom Dorothy describes arriving on 10th June, 1802. '*Coleridge came in with a sack-full of Books etc. and a Branch of mountain ash. He had been attacked by a cow. He came over by Grisdale. A furious wind.*' After Dorothy, Samuel Taylor Coleridge was certainly the most influential person on Wordsworth's life and development as a poet. Much of the story of their association together has already been told in Chapter I and his insistence that Wordsworth was destined to be a great philosophical poet was probably a harmful influence in some of the directions in which he turned Wordsworth's writing.

About his own greatness as a nineteenth century thinker, there can be no doubt. He had formed an acquaintance with Robert Southey before either of them had met Wordsworth and at that time was much occupied with plans for emigrating to America to set up a 'Pantisocracy', an ideal society based upon a form of communism. He and Southey married two sisters but, in spite of their plans, the actual enterprise never developed into anything. At about this time (1795) he met Wordsworth and their meeting developed into the friendship that led to William and Dorothy staying with him at Nether Stowey in Somerset and afterwards moving to Alfoxden House. In the years immediately following this, Wordsworth and Coleridge collaborated on the *Lyrical Ballads* and much of Coleridge's own best verse was written. As with Wordsworth, the excesses of the revolution in France led to a loss of faith in revolutionary fervour for its own sake on the part of Coleridge, and he began to develop a political and religious philosophy much influenced by the thinking of German philosophers which became the foundation for much of the best Anglican thought of the latter part of the nineteenth century.

Writing in *The Prelude* of the mental struggle that his experiences in France induced in him, Wordsworth pays tribute to the joint influences of his sister and Coleridge and how they shared with Nature the task of helping him to draw his ideas into some sort of unity again:

> *Ah! then it was*
> *That thou, most precious Friend! about this time*
> *First known to me, didst lend a living help*
> *To regulate my Soul, and then it was*
> *That the beloved Woman in whose sight*
> *Those days were passed, now speaking in a voice*
> *Of sudden admonition—like a brook*
> *That does but* cross *a lonely road, and now*
> *Seen, heard and felt, and caught at every turn,*
> *Companion never lost through many a league—*
> *Maintained for me a saving intercourse*
> *With my true self; for, though impaired and changed*
> *Much, as it seemed, I was no further changed*
> *Than as a clouded, not a waning moon:*
> *She, in the midst of all, preserved me still*
> *A Poet, made me seek beneath that name*
> *My office upon earth, and nowhere else;*
> *And, lastly, Nature's self, by human love*
> *Assisted, through the weary labyrinth*
> *Conducted me again to open day,*
> *Revived the feelings of my earlier life,*
> *Gave me that strength and knowledge full of peace*
> *Enlarged, and never more to be disturbed,*
> *Which through the steps of our degeneracy,*
> *All degradation of this age, hath still*
> *Upheld me, and upholds me at this day . . .*[1]

After their estrangement, the old relationship between Wordsworth and Coleridge was never fully restored but, in due course, Coleridge's son, Hartley, came to live at Ambleside and frequently walked with Wordsworth and his daughter Dora, around Grasmere. The two of them walking together were the subject of a famous cartoon by Mulcaster which now hangs in the Wordsworth museum at Grasmere and when Hartley died in 1849, he was buried in the churchyard at Grasmere next to the plot that was already reserved for Wordsworth's own grave.

After Wordsworth and Coleridge, the other writer often thought of as belonging to the 'Lake school' is Robert Southey. His early connection with Coleridge has already been mentioned. He, too, was among the young radical writers who welcomed the French Revolution and all that it stood for. He came to live at Keswick with the Coleridges and became Poet Laureate in 1813,

Caricature of Wordsworth and Hartley Coleridge by J. P. Mulcaster, 1844
(Reproduced by courtesy of the Trustees of Dove Cottage)

a post that had been offered to Walter Scott. His later rejection
of his old revolutionary beliefs was even more pronounced than
that of Wordsworth and Coleridge and he was attacked, like
them, by later writers for this act of betrayal, as it seemed to
them. In his *A Vision of Judgement* (1821) he wrote a poem in
praise of the dead George III and this was savagely and
effectively parodied by Byron in his *The Vision of Judgement*
(1822) which gives a good picture of how the later generation of
radical writers tended to see their forebears. Byron was, of
course, almost a contemporary but unlike most of his generation
never compromised with his belief in radicalism and had only
contempt for those who, in his eyes, had sold themselves for
fame and the support of the establishment.

Foremost amongst Wordsworth's many literary friends was
Sir Walter Scott (1771–1832), who was a highly successful
author and an early convert to the revival of the Gothic, a cult

consisting of an interest in the mysterious and the mediaeval, seen very much from a romanticizing perspective.

Both Wordsworth and Coleridge had great admiration for the personal qualities of Scott. When he got seriously into debt as the result of the collapse of a publishing scheme in which he was engaged, he worked himself to a standstill in spite of chronic ill-health, refusing a government pension (as well as the Laureateship) and eventually paid off all his debts. Amongst his poems Wordsworth gives us many pictures of his visits to Scotland, often to see Scott, and the visitor today who uses, for example, his *Yarrow Revisited* (an account, in a sequence of poems, of a tour in Scotland and the Border Country in 1831) as a virtual guidebook to his own wanderings through that countryside is struck, as always, by the accuracy of Wordsworth's observations and the similarity of much of the countryside to the Vale of Grasmere. In the Borders, the poet must have felt himself very much at home. These splendid small poems act as 'memorials' of the visit, often suggested by things that had caught his eye and perhaps serving a very similar purpose to snapshots today in evoking, at a later stage, a scene that had impressed itself and given pleasure.

Scott also travelled south to visit the Wordsworths and was a visitor to Dove Cottage at Grasmere. He appears not to have entirely appreciated the frugal nature of life in that home, however, and there are stories told locally of how he was in the habit of slipping out of his bedroom window in the morning to go down the road to the 'Swan' where he got a better breakfast than the porridge left over from the night before that was the regular early morning fare dished up by Dorothy. He is also supposed to have gone to the 'Swan' for a dram of whisky in the mornings since there was little opportunity for such indulgences in the home of the 'simple water-drinking bard', as Wordsworth described himself.

Among other visitors to Dove Cottage was Thomas de Quincey, who became its tenant when the Wordsworths left it. At first he was a great friend of the Wordsworth family but they became less friendly when he gave way to the habit of taking opium and when he also married Margaret Simpson, the daughter of a local dalesman who had borne him an illegitimate child. De Quincey was very angry about the disdain with which the Wordsworths appeared to regard his wife and although his *Recollections of the Lakes and the Lake Poets*, published as articles in the *Edinburgh Magazine* 1834-40, are always lively and amusing reading, they are often ungenerous to his former friends, especially to Coleridge. However, the *Recollections* are full of entertaining and revealing anecdotes such as the following, showing Wordsworth's way with new books:

> *Wordsworth lived in the open air: Southey in his library*
> *... Southey had particularly elegant habits (Wordsworth called them finical) in the use of books. Wordsworth, on the other hand, was so negligent, and so self-indulgent in the same case, that, as Southey, laughing, expressed it to me some years afterwards, when I was staying at Greta Hall on a visit—'To introduce Wordsworth into one's library is like letting a bear into a tulip garden.' What I mean by self-indulgent is this: generally it happens that new books baffle and mock one's curiosity by their uncut leaves...On a level with the eye, when sitting at the tea-table in my little cottage at Grasmere, stood the collective works of Edmund Burke ... Wordsworth took down the volume; unfortunately it was uncut; fortunately, and by a special Providence as to him, it seemed, tea was proceeding at the time. Dry toast required butter; butter required knives; and knives then lay on the table; but sad it was for the virgin purity of Mr Burke's as yet unsunned pages, that every knife bore upon its blade testimonies of the service it had rendered. Did that stop Wordsworth? Did that cause him to call for another knife? Not at all ... he tore his way into the heart of the volume with this knife, that left its greasy honours behind it on every page: and are they not there to this day?*

So much of de Quincey's writing about the 'Lake Poets' has this immediacy and his essays on them are excellent reading for anyone wanting to get a picture of what Wordsworth really seemed like to a contemporary who knew him well.

The most universally loved of their friends appears to have been Charles Lamb who was at school with Coleridge and who met Wordsworth in 1797. In spite of a good deal of personal trouble—his sister, Mary, who was much loved, had recurrent attacks of madness and he had to look after her all her life—he managed to always remain sympathetic and cheerful and he was a perceptive critic of Wordsworth's work both in his personal letters to him and in some of his periodical articles. When he

died in 1834, Wordsworth wrote an epitaph to him which
expresses his feelings for his friend:

> To a good Man of most dear memory
> This Stone is sacred. Here he lies apart
> From the great city where he first drew breath,
> Was reared and taught ; and humbly earned his bread.

Lamb is best known today for the periodical essays that he
wrote under the name of Elia. It is a form that is not very
fashionable today but these writings still have qualities of charm
and gentle humour and much incidental good sense. Wordsworth
himself knew them and was amused by them and seems to have
had a genuine admiration and affection for their author. One
writing of Lamb's that is less well known than it should be,
alongside the *Tales from Shakespeare* that he wrote jointly with
his sister, is his *Specimens of English Dramatic Poets, who lived
about the time of Shakespeare*, which he published in 1808. This
contains extracts, with critical comments upon, about ninety
scenes from plays by contemporaries of Shakespeare and was one
of the first books to awaken the reader to the many other
important dramatists of Shakespeare's time. In this pioneering
work, he shows that he had similar interests in the world of the
past to those shown by the other members of the Wordsworth
circle which perhaps unified them as a group more than any
other single feature. Lamb was not afraid to give voice to adverse
criticisms of Wordsworth when he thought them justified and, as
usual, Wordsworth tended to react ungenerously to such
comment. Yet despite this, he continued with his friendship
throughout Lamb's life and dedicated *The Waggoner* to him.

One frequently had to work hard to keep up a friendship with
Wordsworth but another of his contemporaries who managed it
was Henry Crabb Robinson who met him in 1808 in London and
who kept very detailed diaries of his friendships with most of the
literary figures of his time. He became close friends with
Wordsworth and visited him in the Lake District as well as
accompanying him on some of his walking tours. His letters and
diaries show that he had a very early and just appreciation of
what Wordsworth's poetry was all about. For example, he writes
in 1802, just after having received a copy of *Lyrical Ballads*:

> There are a few ballads—The Thorn, The Idiot Boy,
> Goody Blake and Harry Gill, *which will rank with the*

*first rate compositions in the Language ... Wordsworth has
the art ... of doing much with simple means. His repetition
of simple phrases, and his dwelling on simple but touching
Incidents, his skill in drawing the deepest moral, and
tenderest interest out of trifles, evince a great master, a
Talent truly Shakespearean ...*

There can have been few readers of the *Ballads* at this stage
who so clearly perceived the true source of their strengths and
who so unerringly picked the right poems to comment upon.
Crabb Robinson's *Diaries* are indispensible as a source of
perceptive and modest comment by someone who obviously
loved and respected Wordsworth as a man as much as he did his
poetry, in spite of having a radical view in politics which led him
to become increasingly out of sympathy with the later more
conservatively-minded Wordsworth.

Another writer who failed to continue his friendship with
Wordsworth in the same way was William Hazlitt. He, too, was a
friend of Charles Lamb and, in *My First Acquaintance with
Poets*,[2] he tells of his meeting with Coleridge and Wordsworth:

*The next day Wordsworth arrived from Bristol at
Coleridge's cottage. I think I see him now. He answered in
some degree to his friend's description of him, but was more
gaunt and Don Quixote-like. He was quaintly dressed
(according to the costume of that unconstrained period) in a
brown fustian jacket and striped pantaloons. There was
something of a roll, a lounge in his gait, not unlike his own
Peter Bell. There was a severe, worn pressure of thought
about his temples, a fire in his eye (as if he saw something in
objects more than the outward appearance), an intense high
narrow forehead, a Roman nose, cheeks furrowed by strong
purpose and feeling, and a convulsive inclination to laughter
about the mouth, a good deal at variance with the solemn,
stately expression of the rest of his face. Chantry's bust
wants the marking traits; but he was teazed into making it
regular and heavy : Haydon's head of him, introduced into
the Entrance of Christ into Jerusalem, is the most like his
drooping weight of thought and expression. He sat down and
talked very naturally and freely, with a mixture of clear
gushing accents in his voice, a deep guttural intonation, and
a strong tincture of the northern burr, like the crust on
wine. He instantly began to make havoc of the half of a*

Cheshire cheese on the table, and said triumphantly that 'his marriage with experience had not been so unproductive as Mr Southey's in teaching him a knowledge of the good things of this life.' He had been to see the Castle Spectre *by Monk Lewis,`while at Bristol, and described it very well. He said 'it fitted the taste of the audience like a glove.' This* ad captandum *merit was however by no means a recommendation of it, according to the severe principles of the new school, which reject rather than court popular effect. Wordsworth, looking out of the low, latticed window, said, 'How beautifully the sun sets on that yellow bank!' I thought within myself, 'With what eyes these poets see nature!' and ever after, when I saw the sun-set stream upon the objects facing it, conceived I had made a discovery, or thanked Mr Wordsworth for having made one for me! We went over to All-Foxden again the day following, and Wordsworth read us the story of Peter Bell in the open air; and the comment made upon it by his face and voice was very different from that of some later critics! Whatever might be thought of the poem, 'his face was as a book where men might read strange matters,' and he announced the fate of his hero in prophetic tones. There is a* chaunt *in the recitation both of Coleridge and Wordsworth, which acts as a spell upon the hearer, and disarms the judgment. Perhaps they have deceived themselves by making habitual use of this ambiguous accompaniment. Coleridge's manner is more full, animated, and varied; Wordsworth's more equable, sustained, and internal. The one might be termed more* dramatic, *the other more* lyrical. *Coleridge has told me that he himself liked to compose in walking over uneven ground, or breaking through the straggling branches of a copse-wood; whereas Wordsworth always wrote (if he could) walking up and down a straight gravel-walk, or in some spot where the continuity of his verse met with no collateral interruption. Returning that same evening, I got into a metaphysical argument with Wordsworth, while Coleridge was explaining the different notes of the nightingale to his sister, in which we neither of us succeeded in making ourselves perfectly clear and intelligible.*

It was after a discussion with Hazlitt that Wordsworth wrote two of his poems, *Expostulation and Reply* and *The Tables Turned,* and they are an indication of the very real differences in thinking between the two writers. While Hazlitt was staying at Keswick, to visit Coleridge in 1803, he painted portraits of both Wordsworth and Coleridge and these may be compared with his prose description of the two poets. However, Hazlitt was an admirer of Napoleon and became a severe critic in print of Wordsworth's work which led to their growing apart from each other until, in 1815, Wordsworth refused to see Hazlitt on a visit to London and the final break in their relationship resulted. Wordsworth's comment on him maintained that he was '*not a proper person to be admitted into respectable society, being the most perverse and malevolent Creature that ill luck has ever thrown in my way*', and the painter Haydon, in his diary for 1824, recounts an entertaining story told by Wordsworth of Hazlitt's licentiousness*.

Enough has been said in this chapter to give some picture of Wordsworth in his personal relations, well known and knowing most of the major literary figures of his time, but with his relationships often bedevilled by his powerful urge for self-justification and his impatience with those who failed to appreciate his work or who dared to utter adverse criticism of it. But the many accounts that his friends and acquaintances have left of him indicate the striking effect that he had upon his contemporaries as much as a character as a poet. Perhaps one of the most moving accounts is of a meeting at a dinner party given by the painter Haydon at which both Wordsworth and Keats were present, together with many of their friends. In the background of the room where the dinner was given was Haydon's own painting of *Christ's Triumphal Entry into Jerusalem* in which both Keats and Wordsworth appear as spectators. We may most satisfactorily close this chapter with a glimpse at the assembled friends in Haydon's own account of the dinner as given by Rannie in his book *Wordsworth and his Circle*:[3]

> *In all the fun and extravagance Wordsworth heartily joined after his manner. After dinner an inimitable*

---

* 'He was relating to me with great horror Hazlitt's licentious conduct to the girls of the Lake and that no woman could walk after dark, for his "satyr and *beastly* appetites". Some girl called him a black-faced rascal, when Hazlitt enraged pushed her down, "and because, Sir" said Wordsworth, "she refused to gratify his abominable and devilish propensities, he lifted up her petticoats and *smote* her on *the Bottom!*"' (Haydon's *Diary*, 29th March, 1824).

Christ's Triumphal Entry into Jerusalem by Haydon (Reproduced by courtesy of St Gregory Seminary College, Ohio)

intellectual toady — like Wordsworth, a Comptroller of Stamps — turned up, and his platitudes gave Lamb — now more than half-seas-over — a great opportunity. 'Don't you think, sir,' said the new guest to Wordsworth, 'that Milton was a great genius?' The rest, though it has been told so often, must be told yet once more in Haydon's words. 'Keats looked at me, Wordsworth at the Comptroller. Lamb, who was dozing by the fire, turned round and said, "Pray, sir, did you say Milton was a great genius?" "No, sir; I asked Mr Wordsworth if he were not." "Oh," said Lamb, "then you are a silly fellow." "Charles! my dear Charles!" said Wordsworth; but Lamb, perfectly innocent of the confusion he had created, was off again by the fire. After an awful pause, the Comptroller said, "Don't you think Newton a great genius?" I could not stand it any longer. Keats put his head into my books ... Wordsworth seemed asking himself, "Who is this?" Lamb got up, and taking a candle, said, "Sir, will you allow me to look at your phrenological development?" He then turned his back on the poor man, and at every question of the Comptroller he chaunted —

> "Diddle, diddle, dumpling, my son John
> Went to bed with his breeches on."

'The man in office, finding Wordsworth did not know who he was, said in a spasmodic and half-chuckling anticipation of assured victory, "I have had the honour of some correspondence with you, Mr Wordsworth." "With me, sir?" said Wordsworth, "not that I remember." "Don't you, sir? I am a Comptroller of Stamps." There was a dead silence; the Comptroller evidently thinking that was enough. While we were waiting for Wordsworth's reply, Lamb sung out —

> "Hey diddle, diddle,
> The cat and the fiddle."

'"My dear Charles!" said Wordsworth —

> "Diddle, diddle, dumpling, my son John,"

chaunted Lamb, and then rising, exclaimed, "Do let me have another look at that gentleman's organs." Keats and I hurried Lamb into the painting-room, shut the door, and gave way to inextinguishable laughter. Monkhouse followed

*and tried to get Lamb away. We went back, but the
Comptroller was irreconcilable. We soothed and smiled and
asked him to supper. He stayed, though his dignity was
sorely affected. However, being a good-natured man, we
parted all in good humour, and no ill effects followed. All
the while, until Monkhouse succeeded, we could hear Lamb
struggling in the painting-room, and calling at intervals,
"Who is that fellow? Allow me to see his organs once
more."'*

[1]William Wordsworth *The Prelude* (1805 version) Bk X ll 905–30
[2]William Hazlitt 'My First Acquaintance with Poets' published in
The Liberal 1823   [3]D. W. Rannie *Wordsworth and his Circle*
(Methuen, 1907)

8

The Critics and Wordsworth

I

'*Up to 1820 the name of Wordsworth was trampled under foot; from 1820–1830 it was militant; from 1830 to 1835 it has been triumphant.*' De Quincey's famous phrase sums up the tendency of the criticism of Wordsworth in his own time. However, in charting the changes in response to Wordsworth's work in the writings of his contempories we can certainly learn something about the shifting and changing taste of the Romantic sensibility. Wordsworth himself was in no doubt that anything that was genuinely original in poetry had to set about the creation of the taste by which it was to be enjoyed ('*Whatever is too original will be hated at first,*' as De Quincey puts it). He set himself to do precisely this—as well as to elaborate the details of his own poetic theory in the Preface and the various later additions to it that accompanied *Lyrical Ballads.* He also had no doubts both about his own worth and his originality and in this he was strongly supported by many friends whose opinions he could respect and who enabled him to keep going in spite of constant criticism from outside. Nonetheless, one might argue that it was the promulgation of the new poetic as much as the poems themselves that led to the debate that was strongly associated with Wordsworth's work in his lifetime and which has been a continuing debate since.

In fact the first, 1798, edition of *Lyrical Ballads* received reasonable notices. *The Monthly Review* did comment upon the general gloom of the subject matter in its famous summary: '*Each ballad is a tale of woe*' but was otherwise encouraging and complimentary; and Southey is by no means discouraging in his remarks:

> *The experiment, we think, has failed, not because the language of conversation is little adapted to 'the purposes of poetic pleasure' but because it has been tried upon an*

interesting subject. Yet every piece discovers genius; and ill as the author has frequently employed his talents, they certainly rank him with the best of living poets.

Typically, Wordsworth was displeased by this comment and felt that if Southey was not going to write something that would help to sell his books then, as a friend, he ought to have passed the task to someone else. Good notices at this time were of the utmost importance to Wordsworth. The reviewing periodicals were much more widely read than poetry itself and if his name was to get before the public, notices in as many as possible of the large number of periodicals was essential. It could be, in fact, that some of the outspoken nature of the Preface to the second edition of *Lyrical Ballads* was deliberately designed to stir up controversy and get the work talked about. In this it certainly succeeded.

Wordsworth's most implacable enemy as a critic was Jeffrey of the *Edinburgh Review*, who also doubtless saw the values of building up a controversy over the poems. He was sometimes accused of hypocrisy and it was claimed that he had been seen in tears as he read *Lyrical Ballads*, but in print, at any rate, he was totally uncompromising:

> *These gentlemen are outrageous for simplicity; and we beg leave to recommend to them the simplicity of Burns. He has copied the spoken language of passion and affection, with infinitely more fidelity than they have ever done, on all occasions which properly admitted of such adaptations: but he has not rejected the help of elevated language and habitual associations; nor debased his composition by an affectation of babyish interjections, and all the pulling expletives of an old nursery-maid's vocabulary . . . Let them think, with what infinite contempt the powerful mind of Blake would have perused the story of Alice Fell and her duffle cloak . . .*
>
> (author's emphasis)

The phrase to which attention has been drawn by the underlining makes clear the real roots of Jeffrey's objections to Wordsworth and the whole 'Lake school of poetry', as he contemptuously called them. He was fundamentally an old-fashioned reviewer who believed above all in the principle of *decorum*; he was setting out to judge the poetry of the new age by standards that had applied to the eighteenth century's official canons of criticism and which had not been by any means universally accepted in practice even then.

The two major sources of Jeffrey's dislike of Wordsworth's work can be located in two early reviews of his which established a position that he continued in thereafter. In the first, a digression on Wordsworth in a review of Southey in the *Edinburgh Review* in October 1802, he shows the clear class bias on which his literary judgments are based:

> *The language of the higher and more cultivated orders may fairly be presumed to be better than that of their inferiors; at any rate, it has all those associations in its favour, by means of which a style can ever appear beautiful or exalted, and is adapted to the purposes of poetry, by having been long consecrated to its use. The language of the vulgar, on the other hand, has all the opposite associations to contend with; and must seem unfit for poetry, (if there were no other reason,) merely because it has been scarcely ever employed in it.*
>
> *... We may excuse a certain homeliness of language in the productions of a ploughman or a milkwoman; but we cannot bring ourselves to admire it in an author, who has had occasion to indite odes to his college-bell ... The poor and vulgar may interest us, in poetry, by their* situation; *but never, we apprehend, by any sentiments that are peculiar to their condition, and still less by any language that is characteristic of it. The truth is, that it is impossible to copy their diction or their sentiments correctly, in a serious composition; ... not merely because poverty makes men ridiculous, but because just taste and refined sentiment are rarely to be met with among the uncultivated part of mankind.*

The sentiments expressed here are similar to those that led to a tidying up of the uncouthness of the oral tradition of the ballad amongst the earliest collectors. They are the expression of an age in which the only pure tradition for poetry is seen as literary and in which the strength that has always existed in the oral folk literature of England has become ignored. In beginning to recreate the strength of this tradition in literary terms, Wordsworth, even if, at times, his own background and extremes led him to absurdity, was beginning a movement that was to have influence far beyond the Romantic age itself.

The second extract from Jeffrey lays bare the other critical judgment upon which he relies—that of taste, the eighteenth century value of decorum, a sense that certain subjects only are fitting matter for poetry. It occurs in his 1807 review of *Poems in Two Volumes*, a destructive piece of criticism which certainly affected the sales of the book:

> *One great beauty of diction exists only for those who have some degree of scholarship or critical skill. This is what depends on the exquisite* propriety *of the words employed, and the delicacy with which they are adapted to the meaning which is to be expressed. Many of the finest passages in Virgil and Pope derive their principle charm from the fine propriety of their diction ... From this great source of pleasure, we think the readers of Mr Wordsworth are in a great measure cut off ... With Mr Wordsworth and his friends it is plain that their peculiarities of diction are things of choice, and not of accident. They write as they do, upon principle and system; and it evidently costs them much pains to keep* down *to the standard which they have proposed to themselves ... in point of fact, the new poets are just as great borrowers as the old; only ... instead of borrowing from the more popular passages of their illustrious predecessors, they have preferred furnishing themselves from vulgar ballads and plebeian nurseries.*[1]

The whole of this review is worth reading for the light that it throws upon the informed and cultivated taste of the time as expressed by the editor of one of the most influential reviewing journals. It makes clear to what an extent the early work of Wordsworth was a genuine revolution in English poetry. The attacks upon it were as much political in their inspiration as literary: it was the radicalism that went along with the admiration for the revolution in France that was under attack as much as the poems themselves.

Jeffrey continues with the attack thereafter including his famous review of *The Excursion* in November 1814 which is magisterial in its tone of rebuke to the author, now famous and established: '*This will never do! ... The case of Mr Wordsworth, we perceive, is now manifestly hopeless; and we give him up as altogether incurable, and beyond the power of criticism.*' But enough has been quoted already to exemplify the torrent of abuse that was showered upon Wordsworth by hostile critics to which, it must be added, he often replied in good measure, especially in his letters. Indeed, by the time of the review of 1814 the quarrel between Jeffrey and Wordsworth had grown to such an extent on a personal level that any serious argument on either side could no longer be rationally expected. Wordsworth had issued his manifesto with the *Lyrical Ballads* and their Prefaces; now it was for Coleridge to produce a measured and skilful reply to Jeffrey's outburst in Chapters 14–22 of the *Biographia Literaria*, (1817).

Very early on, in his *Essay, Supplementary to the Preface* of 1815, Wordsworth had laid down stringent conditions for a critic whose judgment he would be disposed to accept:

> *Where are we to look for that initiatory composure of mind which no selfishness can disturb? For a natural sensibility that has been tutored into correctness without losing anything of its quickness; and for active faculties, capable of answering the demands which an Author of original imagination shall make upon them, associated with a judgement that cannot be duped into admiration by aught that is unworthy of it?—among those and those only, who, never having suffered their youthful love of poetry to remit much of its force, have applied to the consideration of the laws of this art the best power of their understandings.*

These are high criteria for judgment but the egotism and commercial sense of Wordsworth also needed to be satisfied as is shown in this characteristic and self-congratulatory extract from a letter to his brother of 26th June, 1803:

> *I have had high encomiums on the poems from the most respectable quarters, indeed the highest authorities, both in literature, good sense, and people of consequence in the State. There is no doubt but that if my health should enable me to go on writing I shall be able to command my price with the Booksellers.*

Even up to 1820, there was some compensation for 'being trampled underfoot', it seems.

2

It is illuminating, as well as amusing, to notice the attitude towards Wordsworth frequently adopted by those in the generation that followed immediately upon him. This often found its most penetrating, and perhaps most wounding, expression through parody and there were, of course, elements in the Wordsworthian style that were very susceptible to this treatment. The fundamental critical question remains what is missing from the parodies, what makes Wordsworth so much more than the stylistic tricks alone? The point is well established by comparing any one of the *Lucy* sequence of poems with the following parody by Hartley Coleridge, Samuel Taylor's son:

> *He lived amidst th' untrodden ways*
> *To Rydal Lake that lead ;*
> *A bard whom there were none to praise,*
> *And very few to read.*
>
> *Behind a cloud his mystic sense,*
> *Deep hidden, who can spy?*
> *Bright as the night when not a star*
> *Is shining in the sky.*
>
> *Unread his works—his 'Milk White Doe'*
> *With dust is dark and dim ;*
> *It's still in Longmans' shop, and oh!*
> *The difference to him.*

In particular, if one compares the parody with the original on which it is based, perhaps the most artlessly simple of the whole sequence, one sees that Hartley Coleridge is making a relevant point in relation to the original, though from the opposite standpoint to that which Wordsworth himself would have adopted:

> *She dwelt among the untrodden ways*
> *Beside the springs of Dove,*
> *A Maid whom there were none to praise*
> *And very few to love :*
>
> *A violet by a mossy stone*
> *Half hidden from the eye!*
> *—Fair as a star, when only one*
> *Is shining in the sky.*
>
> *She lived unknown, and few could know*
> *When Lucy ceased to be ;*
> *But she is in her grave, and, oh,*
> *The difference to me!*

The whole point of this poem is contained in the antithesis in the second stanza, in the comparison of the two images of the 'violet' and the 'star'. A violet may shine brightly amongst the moss that half conceals it but it is difficult to discern; only those who are willing to look and who have eyes atuned to what they are looking for are likely to find it. It is tiny and shrinks away from our notice. It is essentially something for the sole individual to find and cherish. By contrast the sole star shining in the sky is a public experience: it stands out and by its uniqueness draws our attention inevitably towards it.

The two images also have another quality common in the poems of Wordsworth at this period: that of a kind of inclusiveness, taking in the whole of the universe and universal Nature. The violet causes us to bend down to the earth to look at it, the star demands our raising our eyes skyward so that, imaginatively, we take in a whole arc starting close at hand and sweeping outwards. The neglected violet, which only a few have

Portrait of Wordsworth in old age by Haydon (National Portrait Gallery, London)

both the patience and discrimination to see, is, nonetheless, for those that *can* see (*'He who hath ears to hear let him hear'*). It is just as fair as the star that draws our attention to it. When Lucy dies, few will even know, fewer still will mourn her death, but for the one person who has known her beauty and responded to it the universe has changed and become poorer, just as it would if a passer-by were to step on the unnoticed violet. In other words, it is our personal response that matters; if one person loved Lucy and is aware of her death that is all that matters. Personal and not public notice is what counts in the end.

Certainly, as this study elsewhere makes clear, Wordsworth was never indifferent to public acclaim. Few poets can have sought fame more and been more pleased when they received it, but he always regarded public recognition as his due. The real worth of his poetry was something that few understood and, embittered though this may have made him at times, Words-worth frequently gives expression to the anger he feels for those who cannot be bothered to read him with the attention he both deserves and demands. The point comes out most clearly in an important letter to Sir George Beaumont, written in February 1808, in which Wordsworth draws attention to the closeness of reading and accuracy needed to appreciate his poetry. He writes of *I wandered lonely as a cloud* or 'The Daffodils', which is still a good example of a poem that we tend to read superficially because of its being too familiar to us. He is commenting upon the reported remarks of a friend of the Beaumonts:

> *'Instances of what I mean,'* says your friend, *'are to be found in a poem on a daisy'* (by the bye, it is on the *Daisy*, a mighty difference) *'and on the daffodils* reflected *in the water'*...*what shall we think of criticism or judgement founded upon, and exemplified by, a poem which must have been so inattentively perused? My language is precise; and, therefore, it would be false modesty to charge myself with blame.*

> Beneath the trees
> Ten thousand dancing in the *breeze*.
> The waves *beside them* danced, but they
> Outdid the *sparkling waves* in glee.

> *Can expression be more distinct? And let me ask your friend how it is possible for flowers to be* reflected *in water where*

there are waves? They may indeed in still *water; but the very object of my poem is the trouble or agitation, both of the flowers and the water. I must needs respect the understanding of everyone honoured by your friendship; but sincerity compels me to say that my poems must be more nearly looked at before they can give rise to any remarks of much value, even from the strongest minds . . .*

. . . The fact is, the English Public *are at this moment in the same state of mind with respect to my poems, if small things may be compared with great, as the French are in respect to Shakespeare; and not the French alone, but almost the whole Continent. In short, in your friend's letter, I am condemned for the very thing for which I ought to have been praised; viz., that I have not written down to the level of superficial observers and unthinking minds. Every great poet is a teacher: I wish either to be considered as a teacher, or as nothing.*

We shall be returning to the 'Daffodils' in a different context later. But this clear statement by the poet demonstrates the importance he placed upon the accuracy both of observation and of language in his work and his conviction that his particular greatness would only be understood by the reader qualified to read him—and of these there were very few, even amongst his closest friends. Hartley Coleridge's parody is entertaining and works at a superficial level but it quite misses the point that the original poet is making.

The same point is equally true of Shelley's brilliantly sarcastic parody in *Peter Bell the Third* (October 1819), which is well worth reading for its own sake:

He also had dim recollections
    Of pedlars tramping on their rounds;
Milk pans and pails; and odd collections
Of saws and proverbs; and reflections
Old parsons make in burying grounds.

But Peter's verse was clear, and came
    Announcing from the frozen hearth
Of a cold age, that none might tame
The soul of that diviner flame
    It augured to the Earth.

For language was in Peter's hand
Like clay while he was yet a potter ;
And he made songs for all the land,
Sweet both to feel and understand,
As pipkins late to mountain Cotter.

Shelley here is making a serious point behind the parody that was to bedevil Wordsworthian criticism for long after, the artificial division of the thinking processes of the poet from the language in which the thought was clothed. It became the received doctrine of the ensuing age that Wordsworth was a simple poet of Nature, that he expressed commonplace thoughts but did so in language which had a majesty of its own in spite of the banal nature of the ideas expressed. We do not have to agree with Coleridge's disastrous view that Wordsworth was especially suited to be a great philosophical poet but we have to take seriously his own claim to be regarded as a 'teacher, or as nothing.' The teacher works by example rather than precept and in the concrete example, such as the 'Daffodils' provides, rather than in the abstract assertions of *The Excursion*, we find the real strength of Wordsworth but we cannot ignore the precision of his ideas without doing him a serious disservice.

The partiality of response suggested here was implicit in the comparative lack of interest in *The Prelude* when Mary Wordsworth published it posthumously in 1850. Here, after all, was the poem on which Wordsworth had laboured for most of his life; if anything is essential to a consideration of his work that poem undoubtedly is. But the reviews were relatively few and superficial. An exception was the *Eclectic* which gave it a serious and perceptive notice but the 1850 version of *The Prelude* had been so tidied up by its author's revisions and the form of its eventual publication that the real complexities and paradoxes of Wordsworth's developing ideas were quite unrecognized by the contemporary readers. The Victorian Wordsworth was a highly selected one, one based, for the most part, upon simple platitudes and pieties, the author above all of *Poems in Two Volumes* and the second volume of *Lyrical Ballads*. The strangeness and oddities of much of the first, 'experimental' volume, and the developing thought of the later Wordsworth can all be conveniently ignored. The conventional view of Wordsworth, which still holds sway in popular estimation today, was that summed up in the *Eclectic* in its review of Christopher Wordsworth's *Memoir*, also of 1850:

*He did not sufficiently sympathise with the doings of society,
the fulness of modern life, and the varied passions, unbeliefs,
sins and miseries of modern human nature ... He saw at
morning, from London bridge 'all its mighty heart' lying
still: but he did not at noon plunge artistically into the thick
of its throbbing life, far less sound the depth of its wild
midnight heavings of revel and wretchedness, of hopes and
fears, of stifled fury and eloquent despair ... He has upon
the whole stood aside from his time—not on a peak of the
past—not on an anticipated Alp of the future, but on his
own Cumberland highlands—hearing the tumult and
remaining still, lifting up his life as a far seen beacon fire,
studying the manners of the humble dwellers in the vales
below—'piping a simple song to thinking hearts', and
striving to waft to brother spirits the fine infection of his
own enthusiasm, faith, hope and devotion.*

This is a Wordsworth who has been neatly accommodated to
the spirit of the 1850s—it may be a picture that has some truth
so far as the Wordsworth who had died that year was concerned,
but it misses out the essential core of the story. The birth of
modern Wordsworthian criticism may be seen in the developing
awareness of those elements that the Victorians left out of
account.

3

In his very helpful introduction to his collection of
critical essays on Wordsworth[2] in the Twentieth Century Views
series, M. H. Abrams locates the two persistent alternative views
of Wordsworth in the rival estimates of Matthew Arnold and
A. C. Bradley. Arnold's essay, published in 1879 as the introduction to his edition of *The Poems of Wordsworth*, has certainly been
influential, at least as much for the selection of poems that he
presented as for the critical comments themselves. He established
for Wordsworth, as he did for many other writers, a valuation
that is still a large part of the orthodoxy of Wordsworthian
criticism. It is to Arnold that we owe the concept of the 'great
decade' for example:

*It is no exaggeration to say that within one single decade ...
between 1798 and 1808, almost all his really first-rate work
was produced ... To be recognized far and wide as a great*

*poet, to be possible and receivable as a classic, Wordsworth
needs to be relieved of a great deal of the poetical baggage
which now encumbers him.*

Arnold elevates the distinction between content and style in
Wordsworth into a critical principle:

*His poetry is the reality, his philosophy ... is the illusion.
Perhaps we shall one day learn to make this proposition
general, and to say: Poetry is the reality, philosophy the
illusion. But in Wordsworth's case, at any rate, we cannot
do him justice until we dismiss his formal philosophy ...*

*Nature herself seems, I say, to take the pen out of his hand,
and to write for him with her own bare, sheer, penetrating
power. This arises from two causes: from the profound
sincereness with which Wordsworth feels his subject, and
also from the profoundly sincere and natural character of
his subject itself. He can and will treat such a subject with
nothing but the most plain, first-hand, almost austere
naturalness. His expression may often be called bald, as, for
instance, in the poem of* Resolution and Independence; *but
it is bald as the bare mountain tops are bald, with a baldness
that is full of grandeur.*

We may convincingly argue, with Abrams, that the creation of
'the simple Wordsworth' was very largely that of Arnold but the
work in the twentieth century studies of Wordsworth of critics
such as Helen Darbishire and John Danby convinces us that even
'the simple Wordsworth' requires study and elucidation for a full
understanding.

Such a reading is, however, at best partial, and, at worst,
misleading. In his 1909 *Oxford Lecture on Poetry*, A. C. Bradley
corrected the Arnoldian perspective and, in so doing, laid a
foundation for the other strand of Wordsworth criticism in the
twentieth century. He quotes extensively from Arnold's introduction and comments:

*Now we may prefer the Wordsworth of the daffodils to the
Wordsworth of the yew-trees, and we may even believe the
poet's mysticism to be moonshine; but it is certain that to
neglect or throw into the shade this aspect of his poetry is
neither to take Wordsworth as he really was nor to judge his
poetry truly, since this aspect appears in much of it that we*

cannot deny to be first rate ... Arnold wished to make Wordsworth more popular; and so he was tempted to represent Wordsworth's poetry as much more simple and unambitious than it really was, and as much more easily apprehended than it ever can be.

Bradley does not deny the existence of the Wordsworth that Arnold describes, but he challenges the notion that this is all there is to Wordsworth or that this alone is the Wordsworth who matters; his Wordsworth is one of complexities, of contradictions of thought, style and subject-matter:

All poetic experience is, broadly speaking, of two different kinds. The perception of the daffodils as dancing in glee, and in sympathy with other gleeful beings, shows us a living, joyous, loving world, and so a 'spiritual' world not a merely 'sensible' one. But the hostility to sense is no more than a hostility to mere sense: this 'spiritual' world is itself the sensible world more fully apprehended: the daffodils do not change or lose their colour in disclosing their glee. On the other hand, in the kind of experience which forms our present subject, there is always some feeling of definite contrast with the limited sensible world. The arresting feature or object is felt in some way against *this background, or even as in some way a denial of it. Sometimes it is a visionary unearthly light resting on a scene or on some strange figure. Sometimes it is the feeling that the scene or figure belongs to the world of dream. Sometimes it is an intimation of boundlessness, contradicting or abolishing the fixed limits of our habitual view. Sometimes it is the obscure sense of 'unknown modes of being', unlike the familiar modes. This kind of experience, further, comes often with a distinct shock, which may bewilder, confuse or trouble the mind. And, lastly, it is especially, though not invariably, associated with mountains, and again with solitude.*

Bradley goes on to illustrate each of these statements by analysis of appropriate passages from Wordsworth and it is interesting that the first extensive passage that he quotes is the famous 'stolen boat' episode from *The Prelude*, in this way setting up a precedent for future commentators. Above all, it is the 'intimations' in Wordsworth, the containing of paradoxes and contradictions that Bradley finds impressive, that he should at one time be both pre-eminently the poet of community and the poet of solitude almost as if he apprehends the one through the knowledge of the other. It is with this that *'everything in Wordsworth that is sublime or approaches sublimity has, directly or more remotely, to do with ... And without this part of his poetry Wordsworth would be "shorn of his strength", and would no longer stand, as he does stand, nearer than any other poet of the nineteenth century to Milton.'*

Bradley was, of course, like many other commentators who succeeded him, reinterpreting the Wordsworthian 'system' in terms of his own philosophical interests. We know that in his work as a whole he was a follower of Hegel and believed that the essence of art was the reconciliation of opposites, the fusing together into a unity of seemingly irreconcilable positions. It was natural, therefore, that he should find in paradox the key to his reading of Wordsworth. But in placing stress upon a philosophical Wordsworth, in re-emphasizing the complexity of the poetry and recognizing that there was more to the work of the poet as a whole than the poems of the 'great decade', Bradley redresses the false estimate that Arnold gave and opens up the debate that has continued to dominate Wordsworthian studies to the present day.

Apart from the interesting developments of stylistic criticism that has concerned itself above all else with a close analysis of the texture of Wordsworth's language, such as we see pre-eminently in Jack Jones' *The Egotistical Sublime*[3] and the work of such poet-critics as Donald Davie, it has tended to be those critics who have explored Wordsworth in terms of the thought as well as the feelings of the poems who have made the most significant twentieth century contributions. They tend to agree with Bradley that without such considerations 'Wordsworth is not Wordsworth'. For them, like him, *'the road into Wordsworth's mind must be through his strangeness and his paradoxes, and not round them.'* Those who take this view have found some critical authority from Wordsworth himself in *The Essay, supplementary to the Preface of 1815* in which the complexity of the poetic experience, its quasi-religious nature is explored. But the best justification for accepting a complex view of Wordsworth is the total Wordsworthian canon itself; we cannot ignore the later works any more than we can the later life in our search for a simple interpretation of a complex man and poet. The one thing we can know for certain about Wordsworth is that he was constantly changing and adapting both his thought and his style as he and his circumstances changed and developed. Any one approach is likely to prove illuminating but limiting. The best commentator on Wordsworth remains the poet himself and by exploring the development of the thought and feeling in his major writings, of criticism as well as poetry, we are most likely to approximate to an understanding of what his work is all about.

[1] Quoted in P. Hodgart and T. Redpath *Romantic Perspectives* (Harrap, 1964) [2] M. H. Abrams *Wordsworth* ('Twentieth Century Views' Prentice-Hall, 1972) [3] John Jones *The Egotistical Sublime* (Chatto and Windus, 1954)

Chronology

1770	Birth of Wordsworth at Cockermouth (7th April)	
1771	Birth of Dorothy Wordsworth	
1779	Wordsworth goes to Hawkshead Grammar School	
1788	At St John's College, Cambridge until 1791	
1789	Long vacation spent in walking tour of France and Switzerland	Storming of the Bastille (14th July); French Revolution begins.
1790		Burke's *Reflections on French Revolution* published
1791	Returns to France. Becomes politically involved through meeting Beaupuy. Falls in love with Annette Vallon.	
1792	Birth of illegitimate daughter, Anne-Caroline, to Annette Vallon	Paine's *Rights of Man* published in answer to Burke
1793	Writes *Letter to Bishop of Llandaff* (June)	Execution of Louis XVI (January). England declares war on France (February). 'The Terror' begins in France (September).
1794	In Lake District with Dorothy	Robespierre executed (28th July)
1795	Raisley Calvert dies and leaves Wordsworth £900 thus saving him from earning a living. In London, comes under influence of Godwin and meets Coleridge for first time (August).	

1795	Goes to live with Dorothy at Racedown, Dorset (September until July 1797).	
1797	Coleridge stays with the Wordsworths (5th–28th June). They rent Alfoxden House (July). Walking tour with Coleridge and planning of *Ancient Mariner*.	
1798	Publication of *Lyrical Ballads*	
1799	Rents Dove Cottage, Grasmere	Napoleon becomes First Consul
1800	Dorothy begins *Grasmere Journal*	
1801	2nd (two volume) edition of *Lyrical Ballads*	
1802	Visit to France to see Annette Vallon and Caroline. Publication of 3rd edition of *Lyrical Ballads* with revised and expanded Preface. Marriage to Mary Hutchinson (4th October).	
1804		Napoleon becomes Emperor (May)
1805	Brother, John Wordsworth, drowned. 4th edition of *Lyrical Ballads*.	Battle of Trafalgar
1807	Publication of *Poems in Two Volumes* (May)	
1808	Wordsworths move to Allan Bank, Grasmere. Coleridge accompanies them.	
1810	Publication of *Guide to the Lakes* as anonymous Preface to Wilkinson's *Select Views*. Quarrel with Coleridge.	
1811	Moves to the Rectory, Grasmere	
1812	Reconciled with Coleridge	Napoleon invades Russia
1813	Becomes Distributor of Stamps for Westmorland and moves to Rydal Mount	

1814	Publication of *The Excursion*	
1815	Publication of *Poems, 1815* — first collected edition	Waterloo; end of Napoleonic Wars
1819	Appointed J.P.	Peterloo
1820	New edition of *Poems* (4 volumes). Publication of *Duddon Sonnets*.	
1831	Last meeting with Coleridge	
1832		Reform Bill (opposed by Wordsworth)
1834	Death of Coleridge	
1839	Honorary degree from Oxford	
1842	Publication of *Poems, chiefly of Early and Late Years*. Awarded Civil List pension of £300 a year.	
1843	Appointed Poet Laureate	
1849	Final edition of *Collected Poems* published	
1850	Dies (23rd April) at Rydal Mount. Publication of *The Prelude*.	
1855	Death of Dorothy Wordsworth	
1859	Death of Mary, Wordsworth's wife	

Bibliography

EDITIONS

The editions edited by E. de Selincourt and H. Darbishire of *The Poetical Works of William Wordsworth* (in 5 volumes) and *The Prelude* (Clarendon Press, 1959) are the standard editions. For ease of access, the two volume edition of the *Poetical Works* in the 'Penguin English Poets' series and J. C. Maxwell's edition of *The Prelude* (a parallel text of the two versions), also published by Penguin, are strongly recommended.

The *Prefaces*, along with other important critical texts that may be useful for comparison, are available in D. J. Enright and E. de Chickera *English Critical Texts* (Oxford University Press, 1962). It also contains the relevant sections of Coleridge's *Biographia Literaria*.

Strongly recommended also is E. de Selincourt's edition of *Wordsworth's Guide to the Lakes* (Oxford University Press, 1977).

There is a very useful edition of Dorothy Wordsworth's *Journals*, edited by Mary Moorman (Oxford University Press, 1971).

LIFE

Mary Moorman's two volumes, *William Wordsworth, the Early Years* (1957) and *Wordsworth's Later Years* (1965), both published by the Clarendon Press, are the standard sources for the life of Wordsworth, and Herbert Read's *Wordsworth* (Cape, 1930) is at least as much biographical as critical. As we have already seen, it tends to over-emphasize Wordsworth's relationship with Annette Vallon but it is all the same a highly readable account which does succeed in making Wordsworth come alive as a human being.

HISTORY & BACKGROUND
As general guides to the history of the period, the two volumes in the 'Pelican History of England' by J. H. Plumb (*England in the Eighteenth Century*) and by D. Thomson (*England in the Nineteenth Century*) are strongly recommended. Franklin L. Ford's *Europe, 1780–1830* (Longman, 1970) is a useful and readable account of the period of the French Revolution and Napoleon. F. E. Halliday *Wordsworth and His World* (Thames and Hudson, 1970) is very readable but is especially remarkable for the number and quality of its illustrations. A. S. Byatt *Wordsworth and Coleridge in their Time* (Nelson, 1970) has been of considerable help in preparing this book and has chapters on daily life, the literary world and landscape, amongst others, which will be found very helpful. It, too, is well illustrated.
Thomas de Quincey's *Reminiscences of the English Lake Poets* (Dent, 1961) are lively, and often amusing, reading and William Hazlitt's *The Spirit of the Age* (Oxford University Press), though more difficult, gives a useful perspective on the period.

CRITICISM
It is impossible to give a detailed bibliography of Wordsworthian criticism here and in its profusion it would be of very little use to the readers for whom this book is intended. The most useful first source is the *Penguin Critical Anthology of Criticism on Wordsworth* edited by Graham McMaster (1972) which contains a remarkably full selection of extracts from the critics, grouped under 'Contemporaneous Criticism' (an especially valuable section), 'The Developing Debate', and 'Modern Views'. It also contains a very full bibliography.
The selection that follows is a brief guide to some of the more readable works of criticism alongside some that are of fundamental importance in having trod new ground in our understanding of Wordsworth.
Margaret Drabble's *Wordsworth* in Evans Brothers' 'Literature in Perspective' series (1966) is useful as it is short, readable and concentrates upon exploring Wordsworth as writer through a discussion of many of the poems in detail.

J. F. Danby *The Simple Wordsworth* (Routledge & Kegan Paul, 1960) and Helen Darbishire *The Poet Wordsworth* (Oxford University Press, 1950) with, at times, sharply opposed views are by now classics of Wordsworth criticism and are also short and easy to read in spite of the scholarship that lies behind them.

Along with the already mentioned book by Herbert Read should be placed F. W. Bateson's *Wordsworth—a re-interpretation* (Longman, 1956) which also adopts a quasi-biographical approach to the critical exercise. Bateson makes a good deal of Wordsworth's feeling for and relationship with his sister but in spite of some extravagances the book contains useful insights.

The two earlier classics of Wordsworthian criticism that ought to be at least consulted are Matthew Arnold's introduction to his 1879 edition of Wordsworth's *Poems* and A. C. Bradley's lecture on him in *Oxford Lectures on Poetry* (1909). Both of these are conveniently reprinted in the McMaster book already mentioned. Alongside them should be placed another, though later, classic work of criticism, Herbert Grierson's *Milton and Wordsworth* (Cambridge University Press, 1937) which looks at the 'prophetic' element in Wordsworth's poetry. Much more difficult but of fundamental importance in introducing a totally new critical method is John Jones *The Egotistical Sublime* (Chatto and Windus, 1954).

On the critical writings of Wordsworth himself in the *Prefaces* and elsewhere, W. J. B. Owen's two books, *Wordsworth's Preface to Lyrical Ballads* (Rosenhilde and Bagge, 1957) and *Wordsworth as Critic* (Oxford University Press, 1969) will be found helpful, if perhaps a little over-detailed in their treatment.

Finally it should be mentioned that there are two other excellent critical anthologies, one on *Lyrical Ballads* and the other on *The Prelude*, both published in the Macmillan 'Casebook' series, that form useful supplements to McMaster and contain almost everything of interest that he has had to omit for reasons of space.

Audio-Visual Material

The National Committee for Audio-Visual Aids in Education publish a series of multi-media kits to link with *Authors in their Age*, consisting of filmstrip, cassette and notes. The Wordsworth one especially explores his poetry in relation to its background in the Lake District and uses the poems themselves as the basis for the narration. Full details can be obtained from 33 Queen Anne Street, London W1M 0AL.

To See

First and foremost one must come to the Lake District, of course, which is essential if there is any possibility of reaching it—the filmstrip mentioned above is an alternative but, inevitably, a very poor one. Grasmere is the centre of the Wordsworth country and all the major sites are within a few miles. Both Dove Cottage and Rydal Mount are now open to visitors and are well furnished with portraits and items from Wordsworth's own time. Dove Cottage has alongside it a Wordsworth Museum that contains much of interest including many of the original manuscripts.

While in Grasmere, do not fail to visit the church to see the graves of Wordsworth and his sister and to walk extensively with Wordsworth's *Poems* as your guide-book. Dove Cottage also produces a series of slides that show, amongs other things, the garden that Wordsworth made and these may also make a substitute for those unable to visit Grasmere itself.

St John's College, Cambridge is open to visitors and the statue of Newton in Trinity College can still be seen as Wordsworth saw it. Both the National Gallery and the Tate Gallery in London have many examples of the art of the period which will help to illuminate the concept of the picturesque, and the National Portrait Gallery, also in London, has several examples of portraits of Wordsworth's contemporaries.

A good guide to the Lake District with particular reference to Wordsworth and his circle is Hunter Davies's *A Walk Around the Lakes* (Weidenfeld, 1979), which links the topographical background with the life of the major Lake poets.

Index

Page numbers in italics refer to illustrations,
n indicates footnote